LLEWELLYN'S
Little Book of
DRAGONS

Shawn MacKenzie (North Bennington, VT) had her first Dragon encounter when she was four years old, when she happened upon a copy of *The Dragon Green* by J. Bissell-Thomas. A sci-fi/fantasy writer, she is an avid student of myth, religion, philosophy, and animals real, imaginary, large, and small.

LLEWELLYN'S
Little Book of
DRAGONS

SHAWN MACKENZIE

LLEWELLYN PUBLICATIONS
WOODBURY, MINNESOTA

FIRST EDITION
First Printing, 2020

Cover cartouche by Freepik
Cover design by Shira Atakpu
Interior art by Llewellyn Art Department

Llewellyn Publications is a registered trademark of Llewellyn Worldwide Ltd.

Library of Congress Cataloging-in-Publication Data (Pending)

Llewellyn Worldwide Ltd. does not participate in, endorse, or have any authority or responsibility concerning private business transactions between our authors and the public.

All mail addressed to the author is forwarded, but the publisher cannot, unless specifically instructed by the author, give out an address or phone number.

Any internet references contained in this work are current at publication time, but the publisher cannot guarantee that a specific location will continue to be maintained. Please refer to the publisher's website for links to authors' websites and other sources.

Llewellyn Publications
A Division of Llewellyn Worldwide Ltd.
2143 Wooddale Drive
Woodbury, MN 55125-2989
www.llewellyn.com

Printed in China

For my father, Warren MacKenzie,
the most spectacular Dragon I've ever known.
He gave me the world.
I wish I had written faster.

Contents

Tips

Acknowledgments

My profound thanks for their support and wisdom to my friends and fellow scribes, John Goodrich, Brandon Ayre, John Orzehowski, Tai King, and Karen Sanderson.

Through the years they've followed me into Dragon Country, suspending disbelief with wit, patience, and blue pencils at the ready.

To Lee, who helped remind me of joy in the dark times.

And to Marge, who was there.

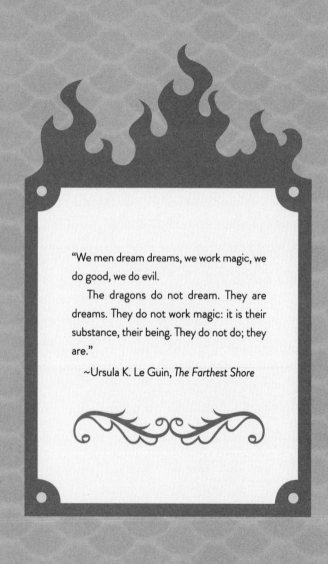

"We men dream dreams, we work magic, we do good, we do evil.

The dragons do not dream. They are dreams. They do not work magic: it is their substance, their being. They do not do; they are."

~Ursula K. Le Guin, *The Farthest Shore*

INTRODUCTION

Long before our ancestors scampered onto the *Homo sapiens* branch of the evolutionary tree, there were all manner of beasts in the world. Land, sea, and air were rife with creatures larger, stranger, more unworldly than the most fervid imagination can conjure. Over millennia, we took those creatures and turned them into a motley array both divine and terrible. From our fears and dreams, we molded them into the stuff of myth and legend, heroics and nightmares; gods and monsters with barely a hair's difference between them. No surprise there. Given the ebb and flow of religious tides, one person's deity becomes another's daemon—and vice versa—in the flick of the Jabberwock's tail. The world,

sublime or beastly, monstrous gods or godly monsters, the universe, as Eden Phillpotts said, "is full of magic things, patiently waiting for our senses to grow sharper" (*A Shadow Passes*, 1918).

And there, with a fiery snort and the patience of Job, are Dragons.

Fantastic, ubiquitous Dragons are without peer among cryptozoological species. They are myth and mystery, muscle and might. They are old magic and new wisdom, playful courtesy and fierce abandon. With gnash of fang and deafening roar, they unleash inferno and flood, raise mountains and carve rivers. With thundering shock and blinding awe, they stoke reverence and fear. Dark and light, victims to saints and advisors to kings, Dragons epitomize the dichotomy of the human condition and guide our existence, inside and out. Through the years they may have exchanged their supernal luster for a more nefarious monster mien, but they can still make us feel small, even irrelevant. They can still trigger adrenaline rushes and inspire us to heights of good and evil. And they fly. Never forget that they fly.

How can we not be captivated by Dragons? Young or old, scientist or fantasist, how can any, save the most timidly prosaic among us, not want to understand their lives and share their company? Dragons are mirrors held up to humanity. They show us at our best and our worst, and teach us—if we're willing to listen—that we too can rise above the mundane and shine like beacons in the dark. We become more human for having known them.

Know Dragons? Absolutely—up close and very personal. But how?

There is the saying among cryptozoologists that the fabulous need us less than we need them. That we are chosen rather than choosing.

On a day more than half a century ago, I was blessed to be chosen by a Dragon. He was Dragon Green, the titular hero emerging from a sea of whimsical prose by J. Bissell-Thomas. He was a wondrously spiky-wiky Dragon if ever I knew one (and I've known a few). Fearless from the moment he hatched in the heat of the Kalahari Desert, he grew up curious and proud, irreverent and lovingly loyal to a fault. He shimmered like a sun-soaked emerald, suffered no fools gladly or otherwise, and when he spread his spinnaker wings, the heavens were his playground. And though his etiquette was understandably dragonish, he had a moral compass that would put most humans to shame. He wasn't perfect, but he was exemplary—a Dragon to be admired and treasured.

> Come at Dragons
> with open minds. Come
> at them with open hearts.
> Come at them with curiosity
> and joy. Simply believe.

Ever since that fateful encounter, I've kept Dragons close. I've studied them, cared for them, and written about them at length. They in turn have kept me safe from daemons of the dark and devils of despair with fire, fang, and chimerical tails. They've taught and reminded me daily that there is so much more to the universe than most of us ever see.

I like to think this is the essence of Dragon Studies— aka cryptoherpetology.

Of course, such a vast, ever-expanding field is beyond the scope of this one little book. (The name alone is a mawful. "Dragon Studies," "Secret Serpent Science," or even "Remarkable Reptile Research" are more user-friendly alternatives.) But what you will find here is a beginning: an exploration of field-specific language and terms, of Dragon species (both True and pseudo-), their history, habitats, and lives. You'll get to look at Dragon-

keeping basics, from sanctuaries and lay-bys to Dragon estates, and enjoy a sampling of Dragon tales, too.

Ultimately, this is an invitation to see with sharper eyes.

Not long ago, I was asked to talk about Dragons with a group of fourth and fifth graders, the perfect age for budding dracophiles. As the kids were settling in, the school librarian pulled me to one side and said very *sub rosa*, "Just don't tell them Dragons are real, all right?" There was a note of pleading in her voice, as if this was something that had come up recently and often. And she sounded a little sad, too. Poor woman, I thought. If only she knew, as Sir Terry Pratchett did, that "you need to believe in things that aren't true. How else can they become?" (Pratchett, *Hogfather*, 2014).

Without answering, I turned to the bright, sharp-eyed kids. I'd barely said hello when a dozen hands shot up: *"Are Dragons real?"*

I smiled my most inscrutable smile—one I picked up from a lovely pearl Dragon from Hokkaido—and said, "Of course."

So, set lingering skepticism aside. Come at Dragons with open minds. Come at them with open hearts. Come at them with curiosity and joy. Simply believe.

And we're off.

Chapter One
LANGUAGE OF DRAGONS

I t is said among people who know—and not a few Dragons—that talking about Dragons is almost as difficult as talking to them.

Enchantments and weyrs. Pyronic sacs and cornicles. Beithirs and tree-skimmers.

By the horns of a green gargoyle, to a novice dracophile's ears, I might as well be speaking bowdlerized basilisk!

Actually, I am speaking the lingua franca of Dragon Country, and, if you wish to explore its byways and lay-bys

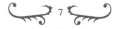

as more than a whistle-stop tourist, 'tis best to learn the basics.

James Baldwin observed that "the root function of language is to control the universe by describing it." Dragon Country is a vast and varied universe, spanning continents and centuries, and full of scaly creatures, great and small. Not easy to control at the best of times, its diversity is both wondrous and daunting and could easily make any meaningful dialogue seem all but impossible. Rather than sound like we're standing waist-deep in the rubble of Babel's tower, serious draconologists and casual dracophiles alike rely on the collected wisdom and specialized vocabulary of the crypto sciences. We are particularly indebted to the fields of cryptozoology and its Dragon-centric offshoot, cryptoherpetology.

But let's start at the beginning.

Crypto Lingo

For those not familiar with the mysterious and arcane, the crypto sciences are, as the words denote, a group of disciplines focusing on matters hidden or secret. Mainstream academics usually dismiss crypto studies as pseudo-, even joke, sciences, a position any good draconologist will vehemently contest, as will devotees of the woodwose, kelpie, fu-dog, and thunderbird. The umbrella field of study for all creatures strange and unusual, from abadas to zaratans (and, naturally, Dragons) is cryptozoology. This is a science which can be traced back to the days of early naturalists such as Aristotle, Pliny the Elder, and Isidore of Seville, all respected scientists and sages of their times. The founders of modern cryptozoology, Bernard Heuvelmans and Ivan Sanderson, were themselves bona fide zoologists with distinguished careers on sanctioned scientific turf. They were also pioneers in a brave new crypto world, looking beyond nature's readily apparent wonders into the eyes of creatures shrouded in ancient lore and disbelief. To the best of their ability, they used rigorous methods of inquiry. Whether pursuing wyverns or aardvarks, they asked questions, made observations, consulted the existing knowledge base, collected and interpreted data, and drew appropriate conclusions. That they were hindered in their studies by their subjects hardly negates their findings. Unfortunately, all this (not to mention the inherent danger in confronting many crypto species, or cryptids, in the wild) carries little weight with those who refuse to accept possibilities beyond their own experience. The myopic see yetis, leshi, sea serpents—Dragons—as mere inventions of human fancy. The cryptozoologist sees them as hidden—often with good cause.

Dragons, naturally, have pride of place in cryptozoological circles. This is due in large part to their heterogeneity and universal presence. I like to think it's also because Dragons are just impossible to resist. Their majestic mystery reaches out and demands we mere mortals sit up and pay attention. Too magnificent and complex to be relegated to a single crypto science, Dragons are what you might call interdisciplinary beings, their study—and the rich language of that study—sprouting from numerous branches of the crypto tree. The most pertinent of these are:

Cryptoherpetology

Also known as Secret Serpent Science, Remarkable Reptile Research, and, simply, Dragon Studies. This is the jumping-off place for serious Dragon lovers and would-be Dragon keepers. It covers the natural and metaphysical aspects of all Dragon species, both True and pseudo-, as well as some non-Dragon hybrids, such as the chimera, and a number of water creatures who fall into the grey area between fish and reptile, like the great fire salamander.

Crypto-anthropology

This is the study of how fabulous creatures affect human cultures. Recently, studies have focused more and more on the social structure within a particular crypto species. Given the intricate nature of Dragon kinship, this new approach has produced a trove of knowledge about interactions within Dragon society.

Cryptomythology

One of the most fascinating, yet often derided, fields, cryptomythology sorts through what is real and what is fancy about crypto species as related in human lore, religion, oral history, and literature. Dragons have an outsized role in the language of their study.

Cryptopaleontology

The science of fossils as it relates to the world of hidden beings is a complicated study. While there is a growing fossil record of lesser dragon species, the absence of True Dragon fossils continues to frustrate cryptopaleontologists no end. Still, they live in hope, and their contribution to theories of draconic evolution are invaluable.

Cryptoveterinary

As the name implies, this is the medical branch of the crypto sciences. Cryptovets focus on diseases and treatments for mundane ailments that may cross over to the mystical as well as those specific to our friends in the crypto kingdom. Dragons, by and large hale and hardy, naturally have little use for medical aid. That said, accidents happen, injuries and illnesses do occur, and Dragon keepers around the world are beholden to these dedicated healers for the care they give our scaly friends in time of need. Given how testy even the most amiable Dragon can be when poked or prodded—let alone one feeling green around the neck furls—these women and men deserve our awed gratitude. Add to that the knowledge of Dragon biology, anatomy, and reproductive science (cryptotheriogenesis) the vets have been able to share, and they are worth their weight in Fafnir's gold.

Out of these disciplines, and their everyday application by Dragon keepers from pole to pole, comes a word-hoard colorful and resplendent in empirical wisdom, tradition, and whimsy—just the way Dragons like it. A complete draconic lexicon would rival the OED in heft, but the following will give you a solid foundation as you begin to navigate the ever-gyring roads of Dragon Country.

Dragons

Crypto species, especially Dragons, come in mythic/cosmic and flesh-time forms.

Cosmic Dragons

In the beginning there was chaos, and out of that chaos arose divine forces both creative and destructive, light and dark. Some of those forces happened to be Dragons. Generally considered mythic today, Cosmic Dragons are as diverse as the people who named them, their temperaments ranging from the benign to the fiercely malevolent. The Creator Dragons recognized that one way or another, their work required sacrifice. They have given a lot to shape and preserve the Universe, and their energy infuses the world to this day. The Destroyer Dragons' work is yet to be done.

Some of the noteworthy Cosmic Dragons are:

AIDO HWEDO: The Cosmic Rainbow Serpent of the Fon people of Africa who was both aide and friend to the Creator, Mawu. After the world was made, Aido Hwedo wrapped her coils tightly round it to hold it together till the end of time.

ALKHA: Fierce Dragon of Siberia's Buriat people. Alkha was so massive his wings covered the heavens.

TIP 1

Finding Dragon Treasure

Rare though they may be, Dragon eggs are occasionally found in the wild. What to do?

- Observe them from a safe distance for at least 24 hours (in case the Queen returns).

- Contact your local Dragon authorities or WAFDE rep. Provide the precise location of your find.

- If you plan on taking the eggs, transport with care to a proper nesting environment. Incubate until hatching day, and voilà! You're a Dragon keeper.

- If unable to take on the responsibilities of Dragon keeping, don't be hard on yourself. Your Dragon authorities will arrange for the care and fostering of the Dragonlets, once born.

When peckish, he would nibble on the sun and the moon only to throw them up again when their heat became too much for him to stomach. Lunar craters are said to be Alkha's tooth marks.

ANANTA: In the Hindu Vedas, Ananta serves as bed and shade for the god Vishnu, who, in turn, is referred to as Ananta-Shayana, or He Who Sleeps on Ananta.

CAMPACTI: Cosmic Dragon of Mexico who, in defeat, made the ultimate sacrifice for creation: from his body—bone, blood, and sinew—the earth was made.

FIRE DRAGON: An amiable Cosmic Dragon of the Huron and Iroquois people, Fire Dragon enjoyed spending time with Chief-of-All-the Earth's young bride, Aetaentsic. This stirred rumors, even laughter, and, when Aetaentsic became pregnant, her husband was convinced she'd been unfaithful with the Dragon. Unleashed, the Chief's green-eyed monster ranted and rampaged, casting his wife out of the heavens and frightening Fire Dragon so far away that he was never heard from again.

GANDAREVA: Cosmic Dragon from Sumer who stretched from the ocean floor to the starry firmament. For all his ferocious ways, Gandareva kept an even more dangerous Dragon in check. Unfortunately, he was slain by Keresapa and the second Dragon was free to destroy the universe.

MINIA: Creator Dragon of the ancient Sahara from whose sacrifice the world was made.

MIÐGARÐSORMR AND NIÐHÖGGER: Destroyer Dragons of the Norse people. Bound for millennia, with the coming of Ragnarök, they break free and ravage the worlds of gods and men.

SOVEREIGN PLUMED SERPENT, KUKULKAN, AND QUETZALCOATL: The feathered Cosmic Dragons of the New World were a colorful lot, starting with Sovereign Plumed Serpent (aka Gucumatz) of the Maya. According to the sacred Maya text, the Popol Vuh, he/she joined with Heart of Sky to bring the world and all its creatures into existence. It took them numerous tries (people were particularly troublesome), but they got it right in the end. With the Creator's job done and not wanting to get bored, Sovereign Plumed

Serpent transformed into Vision Serpent, Kukulkan. He spent his time perched atop the foliate World Tree, bringing civilization to the people and being invoked as a war god when necessary.

When the Maya faded and the Aztecs rose, Quetzalcoatl spread his feathered wings, replacing Sovereign Plumed Serpent and Kukulkan as the Creator Dragon of the Aztec world.

Flesh-Time Dragons

Dragons in the real world are divided into two groups: True Dragons and pseudodragons.

Considered the direct descendants of the Cosmic Dragons, True Dragons, or capital-D Dragons, come in three species: European/Western Dragons; Asian/Eastern Dragons; and Feathered/Southern Dragons. Accept no substitutions.

All others are pseudodragons, or lesser or lowercase-d dragons. Pseudodragons are so numerous that for the armchair cryptoherpetologist, the best way to grasp their complex multiplicity is through behavioral/habitat classification—thus we have diggers, tree-skimmers, house dragons, and water dragons.

We will explore both True Dragons and pseudodragons in greater detail in chapters 2 and 4.

Dragon Being, Dragon Living

As with all things Dragon, the vocabulary of their physiology and sociology is both specific and charming—including "charming," which you'll soon see. In alphabetical order:

Antienne Eclorsion/Birthing Anthem

The song a Queen Dragon and her attendant family sing to spur her eggs to hatch. This is an essential and spectacular part of the birthing ritual. The *antienne eclorsion* is an offshoot of the more general *Carmina Draconium*, or Dragon Song in Latin. (Dragons do love our ancient languages.)

Charming

The ritual grooming of Dragon horns, essential to keeping them sharp and smooth. Hornfels, a tough, fine-grained metamorphic rock, is considered the best honing tool. Unicorns and other horned crypto species are also known to charm. Chances are a few mundane species do it, too.

Cornicles

Small horns found along a Western Dragon's blaze. Unlike a Dragon's large horns, which have myriad uses, not least of which are defensive, cornicles are largely ornamental. Not that they can't inflict injury—any Dragon horn can—but that's not their primary function. Recent studies suggest they play a role in draconic courtship and mating rituals. It is a subject that demands further investigation ... if Dragons allow it.

Enchantments

An enchantment is the basic extended family unit for Dragons. At the height of Dragon dominion, there could be twenty to thirty-five individuals per enchantment. Sadly, they are roughly half that size today.

Fabulae dracones mori

These are the ancient mystic tales of how Dragons die.

Gigantotherm

Any creature, like the largest dinosaurs—and, of course, Dragons—massive enough to maintain a constant and active body temperature even though they are not strictly speaking warm-blooded. This helps explain how Dragons are found in even the coldest, darkest of climates.

Hemorrhagic Hemotoxin

As the name implies, this venom goes straight to the blood. It destroys red blood cells, clotting ability, and, if untreated, leads to internal bleeding, tissue necrosis (an aid to Dragon

digestion), and a slow, painful death. This is the Feathered Dragon's last line of defense. Like mundane vipers but more so, their fangs are able to inject copious amounts of venom. Of course for Dragons, chances are one good dry bite will suffice. Hemotoxins are also used by some of the scrappier pseudodragons such as the lethal aspis, so as the saying goes, "*Caveat spector!*" Let the watcher beware.

Antienne eclorsion. Fabulae dracones mori. Pax loci— Dragons do love our ancient languages.

Himalayan Quad

A Dragon-rich region in the high Himalayas, home to four known weyrs, possibly more.

Ley Lines/Dragon Currents

The electromagnetic grid that crisscrosses the planet. Dragons are very sensitive to ley lines and will take up residence on or near a ley-line nexus whenever possible.

Pangaea

A pre-continental drift super-landmass in the middle of the super Panthalassic Ocean. Long, long ago, small protodragons roamed from one end of the land to another.

Around 175 million years ago, Pangaea splintered and drifted into the continents we know today, and these primitive Dragons drifted with it, establishing their modern global presence.

Passion Ball/Ardor Orb

A gift from a mating Queen to her other half, a passion ball is a draconic aphrodisiac made from tail sheddings, horn filings, amber, honey, and herbs of choice (often parsley). Formed as the spirit moves her, she will then put it by until it's time to share with her mate to ensure a fecund bonding.

Perchloric Acid ($HClO_4$)

Highly corrosive—and flammable—compound believed by some cryptoherpetologists to be a byproduct of a violent Dragon death. It eats through flesh and bone, thus assuring no fossil record is left behind.

Protodragons

The very first hardly-recognizable-as-Dragons Dragons who walked the earth, swam the seas, and filled the skies at the start of draconic evolution. These hardy individuals survived extinction-level events that took out thousands of larger, more imposing species, presaging their descendants' survival instincts and adaptability. Darwin would be proud.

Pyronic Sacs

Anatomical structure essential to the production of Dragon fire. Pyronic sacs are vestigial at birth and only develop fully as a Dragon enters her second year. Recent studies indicate that even non-fire breathers have similar organs though they remain non-functional, much like the human appendix.

Quaternary Dragons

The first modern Dragons, coming into their own in the late Cenozoic Era, roughly two million years ago. Though considerably larger than their twenty-first-century cousins, the Quaternary Dragons were, in other aspects, indistinguishable from the Dragons of today.

Queen

A breeding female Dragon.

Remembrance of Names

Solemn event in the life of every True Dragon when they, quite literally, remember their name. This usually happens in a Dragon's third year, though some youngsters are more precocious than others. For Dragon keepers and their Dragons, it is a time of great celebration.

Sacred Geometry

The study of specific, perfect proportions in the natural world which led geometers to believe there was a Divine Mathematician at work in the creation of the universe. The tenets of sacred geometry have been used in the planning of temples, churches, and the planting of holy labyrinths. One of the foundations of sacred geometry is the Golden Ratio, which can be applied to the structure of chambered nautilii, Romanesco cauliflower, fractals, and all True Dragons. This not only assists in distinguishing True from pseudodragons, but also leads cryptoherpetologists to declare with conviction that Dragons are perfect beings, touched by the Divine Mathematician. They would say they are touched by the Great Dragon.

Sire

A breeding male Dragon.

Weyr

A Dragon community. In the old days, a weyr could easily accommodate 5–7 enchantments. Unfortunately, everything is down-sized today: modern weyrs are home to 2–3 enchantments at most.

Dragon People

It is said that there are two kinds of Dragon people in this world: those who keep them and those who kill them.

Dragon Keepers

Dragon keepers have been around since the days of China's Xia Dynasty ca. 2200 BCE. In their modern incarnation, they have contributed immeasurably to empirical Dragon knowledge and vocabulary, including:

ADOPT-A-DRAGON INITIATIVE (AAD): An outreach program started by the Dragon Conservancy Program. The AAD is modeled after the adoption programs of the World Wildlife Fund, Sierra Club, and the Bears of the World Fosterage Project. It is a way for Dragon lovers around the globe to stay connected to these marvelous creatures and feel like they are contributing to the continuance of Dragon welfare the world over for a modest fee.

DRACOPHILE: A Dragon lover ... like you.

> There are two kinds of Dragon people in this world: those who keep them and those who kill them.

DRACOPHOBE: A Dragon loather . . . not like you.

DRAGON CONSERVANCY PROGRAM (DCP): An offshoot of the World Association for Dragons Everywhere, the DCP is dedicated to preserving Dragons and Dragon habitat for present and future generations, a mission that is increasingly difficult of late. They are behind the Adopt-A-Dragon initiative, among other efforts.

DRAGON LAY-BY: A Dragon-friendly patch of land established for the rest and recreation of itinerant Dragons.

DRAGON SANCTUARIES: Internationally recognized safe havens surrounding every known wild weyr in the world. Though their sovereignty has been challenged in recent years, they are essential for keeping wild Dragons, and the numerous other, often endangered species who share the environments, safe and sound.

FLYING OINTMENT: A medicinal concoction for Dragons who are having a little trouble getting aloft. Though it is a staple in every Dragon keeper's medicine chest, it can be very unstable and must be handled with the greatest of care.

MOLTING BALM: Another medicine-chest requisite, molting balm is a palliative treatment for Dragons having a hard time shedding their skin. It's good for sunburn, too.

PAX LOCI: Peace of the Place. The golden rule in Dragon lay-bys, it guarantees a civil, injury-free stay for all who drop by.

PYROMETRIC CONES: Idiot-proof temperature gauges commonly used by potters and Dragon keepers. They're perfect for monitoring the temperature in a hatching kiln.

TANSTAAFL: There Ain't No Such Thing As A Free Lunch, wise words for Dragons and humans alike.

WEYRSICKNESS/DRAGON DESPONDENCE: An ailment of the spirit which can afflict Dragonlets just out of the egg, especially those who are orphaned or abandoned. The best course of treatment is time, affection, and liberal doses of Weyrsickness Remedy.

WEYRSICKNESS REMEDY: A concoction of bittersweet, forget-me-nots, and a very generous amount of honey. It's an effective anti-depressant

for young Dragons in the throes of post-hatching Dragon despondence.

WORLD ASSOCIATION FOR DRAGONS EVERY-WHERE (WAFDE): A global organization dedicated to the preservation and protection of the world's Dragons. WAFDE is the leading advocate for the inviolate sanctity of Dragon sanctuaries, as well as being responsible for inspecting and licensing Dragon lay-bys. It serves as a resource center for Dragon keepers and dracophiles and works with various nature conservancies to put an end to the poaching of Dragons and the mundane creatures integral to their ecosystems.

Dragon Slayers

Dragons slayers are a sore point among Dragons and the people who love them. Naturally. Numerous as ticks on a badger—and just as bloodthirsty—they are, thankfully, more figures of the past than the present. Historical relics, you might say. And while many of us prefer slayers not be mentioned at all, that would be a grave whitewashing of draconic history. As a rule, Dragons oppose whitewashing.

Through the centuries, the character and accolades afforded a culture's slayers were directly affected by how

a people viewed their local Dragons. In the early days of human civilization, Dragons ruled the earth, controlled the flow of waters and the bounty of field and forest. They were Nature with four legs and wings. And they had names that inspired wonder and fear: Asdeev, Gandareva, Ladon. The humans who stood against them were more than heroes: they were demi-gods and lauded builders of nations. Killing Dragons solidified their royal credentials and guaranteed their place in song and history. This was the time of Gilgamesh, Cadmus, Keresaspa, and Rustam. In the Common Era, especially among Judeo-Christian people, Dragons went from natural forces to satanic ones. Suddenly, a quick route to canonization careered through the nearest Dragon den. George and Martha, Theodore and Catherine, all had Dragon kills on their saintly resumes. The Common Era also saw the rise of Dragons as the target of heroic/knightly quests. Often rationalized as necessities for the safety and security of the human population, many Dragons were pursued as means to the ends of sport and fame. The impact of all this bloodshed on weyrs will be explored further in Chapter 5: A Brief History of Dragons.

While memories of Dragon slayers are horrific and painful, we cannot ignore their dark legacy. It informs

Dragon conservation, present and future, and illuminates paths never to be followed again.

Now, with rudimentary draconic vocabulary in hand, let's venture forward and put it to use.

Chapter Two

DRAGON SPECIES LARGE AND TRUE

Once upon a time—as all good Dragon tales begin—the Earth was one hot mess of a planet. As the eons passed, the world cooled, waters flowed, and land rose from the seas. It was neither an easy nor rapid birthing, by any means. Almost 2.5 billion years passed before there was even enough free oxygen in the atmosphere to sustain anything more than the simplest life forms, and another 1.5 billion until we had a functioning ozone layer. All that time—and since—the Earth was far from static: the continents were literally shifting, oxygen levels rose and fell, and meteors kicked up enough debris to blot out the sun. Wave upon wave of environmental apocalypses wiped out more species than we can even imagine. The Permian Extinction alone (c. 250 million years ago), saw 90–95 percent of all marine life, 70 percent of land flora and fauna, and some 50 percent of insect species disappear. Fortunately, such events were far from instantaneous, lasting for up to a couple of million years. It took less than that long for modern humans to evolve from our ancient, decidedly more apish ancestors, *Australopithecus*. Even the Cretaceous-Paleogene Extinction event that destroyed the last of the dinosaurs (precipitated by a meteor in the Yucatán) lasted some 10,000 years. This relatively leisurely pace left room for adaptation.

Each time, those who could adapt did, and despite all the obstacles in its way, life continued to blossom, swim, amble, and soar in glorious multiplicity.

Dragons have always been adaptable. At home in the sea, on land, and in the air, feeding on plants and flesh, fresh or carrion, they survived the epochal ebb and flow like few species before or since. While cryptopaleontologists may not be able to trace the exact path Dragons took among the branches of the evolutionary tree, they can swear to that, at least.

By the time our earliest human ancestors rose up on two feet and gazed across the savannah, True Dragons—Eastern, Western, and Feathered—were much as they are today. And they ruled.

Eastern Dragons

Lung. Ryu. Naga. Druk. Ryông. Mireu. Three, four, and five toed. Tufted and scaled, thick as a felled sequoia and twice as long, with noble horns and silken whiskers, these were the venerable Dragons of the Far East. In silk and celadon, green jade and red jasper, legend and lore, they followed the sun from the Pacific Rim to the Bosporus Strait. From the steamy jungles of Irian Jaya to the frosty Lena River delta, they frolicked, plumbing the depths of the Kuril Trench and dining on the bounty of the Coral Sea. With claws like back-hoes, they gouged out river beds and basins; their breath shrouded the peaks from Honshu to the Hindu Kush; and when they danced, they roiled the dust of the Gobi into dunes.

While debate lingers in remote corners of draconic academia, the recent consensus among cryptoherpetologists is that Eastern Dragons are the oldest of the True Dragon trio. After the great Permian extinction, the near-empty Panthalassic Ocean was begging for creatures worthy enough to fill the void and surf her waves.

Enter the earliest ancestors of the Eastern Dragon, small at first, but eager to grow. While at home in any environment, like their twenty-first-century descendants, they treated water like a second skin. Through the ensuing millions of years, these protodragons shed their more primitive sea-serpent aspects and evolved into the wondrous Eastern Dragons of today. [Note: This very process is recounted in the stories of Korean Dragons (Mireu), many of whom begin their lives as imugi—lesser, serpentine water dragons who aspire to be real Dragons. It may take thousands of years; it may take catching a yeouiju (fiery orb/meteor) when it falls from heaven. But they persevere. After all, who doesn't want to be a Dragon when they grow up?]

After all, who doesn't want to be a Dragon when they grow up?

By the time early humans were fishing the pristine waters of the Paleolithic Yangtze, Eastern Dragons would have been familiar sights, basking on the banks or playing keep-away with a pod of river dolphins. Tribal shamans embraced

them as deities, divine forces of nature who could control the elements, especially the waters of which they were so fond. In later years, they became counselors to emperors and symbols of power, longevity, and great good fortune. Royalty claimed them, but being their own Dragons, the enchantments preferred the company of the people—farmers and fisher folk, poets and painters—helping with irrigation, terracing, and inspiration.

As tiny villages grew into sprawling megalopolises and inter-tribal squabbles became major wars, the enchantments were pushed to the fringes. Waters once clear are now poisoned and foul and river dolphins have gone the way of the moa. Much as they are still celebrated and worshipped around the globe, the modern world has tipped our Eastern friends back into survival mode. The Dragons have shed their gregarious ways and become cautious, even reclusive. This is particularly true in China where the politics of the region and the subsequent restrictions on foreign travelers have made Dragon studies extremely difficult in the two hundred years since Britain and China fought their opium wars (1839–42; 1856–60). Yet in an increasingly global environment—and Dragons being about as global as they come—cryptoherpetologists are ever hopeful circumstances will change.

Facts and Figures

Most of us know Eastern Dragons through the arts and legends. As celebrated in story, painting, sculpture, and, thanks to the wonders of animation and high-tech CGI, on film, these marvelous beings are viewed as a salmagundi of aspects of the nine blessed animals: lion, snake, stag, hare, cattle, tortoise, fish, tiger, eagle—the quintessential cosmic mash-up. Representations have been detailed enough that an observant dracophile can easily distinguish True Eastern Dragons from wayward kiaus or Mongolian death wyrms. That said, cryptozoologists provide us with the science to help flesh out these anecdotal accounts.

Eastern Dragons are distinguished from their True Dragon kin by three things: long, serpentine bodies, luxurious manes and ankle tufts, and no wings. They have leonine faces, with thick manes framing their noble, velvet-racked heads. Their well-toothed, mustachioed mouths exude a mien of perpetual amusement, as if they are privy to all the secrets (and jokes) of the Universe.

There are three families of Eastern Dragon, most easily distinguished by a count of their toes. The most prevalent are the five-toed Chinese Dragons, aka Imperial Dragons, who are found across the Asian mainland. Four-toed and

three-toed Dragons are endemic to Korea, Japan, Indonesia, and the Pacific islands, and have been sighted along the coastal lands of Southeast Asia. Five-toed Dragons are so numerous, even today, that it is generally believed they were the trunk of the Eastern Dragons' genetic tree, with three and four toes being evolutionary offshoots. Advancements in DNA testing and genome mapping give cryptoherpetologists hope of verifying this theory in the near future.

Within each family you also have the further distinctions of horned/hornless and flying/flightless. Flying Dragons are generally larger than their earthbound kin, reaching up to 30 meters in length; legend has it their ancestors grew twice that size. Flightless Dragons are considered large at about 15 meters long. Of course, even flying Dragons must touch down to feed, breed, and consort with other creatures. When out for a stroll, all Eastern Dragons keep low to the ground. Like fine brushes, their fur tufts transport pollen around their environs. In a time of declining bee populations, they are increasingly necessary to the overall health of their ecosphere.

Though they don't breathe fire like their Western cousins, they are by no means defenseless. Preferring low profiles to confrontation, they are masters of stillness and

camouflage. Their scales take on the luster of their environment: umbers and ochres among the inland diggers, greens and blacks for forest dwellers. Water Dragons are decked out in blues and greens, and Sky Dragons glisten in coats of azure with frosty metallic points. Their ability to fade into their surroundings, coupled with the reverence they inspire, allow Eastern Dragons to travel with relative ease in their homelands. Every so often, however, they do come maw to maw with dangers requiring more drastic measures. Poachers are a continual worry even in China, where the punishment is most severe if caught. But for any who would dare challenge their kind, it should be remembered: Eastern Dragons pack a powerful chomp (frequently envenomed), their claws (in whatever number) can tear through granite as if it were loam, and a flick of their tails can knock an elephant silly (not that they would).

It is curious that for all their magnificent diversity, humans regard the five-toed, horned, flying Sky Dragons as the species ideal. This is reflected in the divine status and imperial protection afforded them through the centuries. Being more egalitarian by nature as well as realizing that a single weyr can encompass a wide variety of individuals, Eastern Dragons see this for what it is: a reflection of human biases rather than draconic reality.

Western Dragons

A mammoth lizard standing square on four tree-trunk legs, with leathery wings, teeth like sabers, and fiery breath hot enough to turn the finest armor to a puddle of slag (don't even ask about its knightly inhabitant!). Their lairs are filled with gold and jewels they protect with a relentless zeal. And when not helping themselves to sheep or cattle, they extort tribute from the local villagers in the form of virgins. This is your stereotypical Western Dragon, or Westie to those who know them. It's also more faërie tale than draconic fact.

Western Dragons are considered the middle child of the True Dragon triad, evolving from savvy wingless protodragons who wandered Pangaea in the shadow of much larger and less adaptable amphibians and reptiles. Where their Eastern relatives filled post-extinction voids in the seas, they filled the open niche on land, rising up the terrestrial food chain. From negligible shoulder nodules, they sprouted wings, increasing their range and avoiding the jaws of earth-bound carnivores. Millions of years passed; surviving meteors, continental drifts, and cataclysms of

monumental proportions, they transformed into the spectacular beings they are today.

Unlike their honored Eastern cousins, Western Dragons have been synonymous with demonic forces, particularly since the Common Era. While adopted by kings and warriors as emblems of power and fierceness, in real life, they have been treated with more fear and loathing than veneration. And as people have known since ancient times (and Dragons long before that), the energy we put out for good or ill comes back to us three-fold. To be more species specific: poke a Dragon and don't be surprised if you get singed—or worse.

The major bone of contention between Western Dragons and *Homo sapiens*—aside from getting caught up in religious symbolism far from their own making—involved land. They had it, we wanted it. In the long history of humans and Western Dragons, 999 times out of 1,000, our kind moved into their territory without so much as a by-your-leave. This was eminent domain at the point of a sword, and Dragons had every right to defend their homes. They were there first, after all; we would do exactly the same if the positions were reversed. And when the promise of epic glory wasn't enough incentive to risk life and limb, chieftains and monarchs appealed to good old human greed: a princess's hand, lands and estates, and, of course, the Dragon's hoard, there for the taking... tempting lures even if accounts of Dragon troves were greatly exaggerated.

Populations grew and villages exploded into towns, towns into cities. Over the years, this meant increased clashes with Dragons that led to vicious cycles of blood and loss. Knight kills Dragon, Dragon's kin kills knight, and on and on until no one is left, or someone has the good sense to sit down and parley a truce. Unfortunately, in the West, the former was usually the case. (More on that in chapter 5.) The increasing contempt in which Western Dragons were held led to the weyr axiom: Call no Unicorn "horse," nor Dragon "lizard"—at least not to their faces.

With the advent of Dragon studies and subsequent surge of draco-phile goodwill toward our calid friends, we're finally respecting Western Drag-ons for the wise and noble beings they are. We have learned that they have nat-urally gregarious dispositions and are curious, to boot. Finding

Call no Unicorn "horse," nor Dragon "lizard"— at least not to their faces.

them more accessible than their Eastern kin, cryptoher-petologists are blessed with considerably more (if still incomplete) knowledge of the species. If we can just rally together and protect the planet we all need, we might be around long enough to really get to know one another.

Facts and Figures

Legends and lore may be wrong about Western Dragon temperaments and habits, but they're surprisingly accurate when it comes to basic physical attributes. Westies are *huge*, an essential factor in discerning True Dragons from some of the larger pseudodragon species, particularly wyverns. Dracophiles also know a quick limb count is the surest way to know with whom you're dealing, and since wyverns can be dangerously ill-mannered, it's always better never to assume. Keep your distance until you know for sure you're dealing with a proper Dragon. Safe is better than dead.

Full-grown Western Dragons are between 25 and 40 feet in length, not counting their tails, which can add approximately 60 more feet to their total. Being proportionate, their wingspans can reach over 100 feet when fully extended. Fortunately, they fold up neatly, allowing for graceful ambles as the spirit moves them. Their

scales are virtually impenetrable and prove an excellent defense against the elements … and many a human foe, too. For purposes of hygiene and pest control—as much as Dragons need it—there is nothing like a long soak in lake or stream, followed by a proper dusting. No tick or mite, however tenacious, can survive a good roll among the dunes.

Tail spades, neck furls, and cornicles are as individual as fingerprints and easier to use than tags or collars when it comes to identifying and tracking enchantments in the wild. While horn similarities can denote kinship, diversity within enchantments, even within a single clutch, are not uncommon. This does not imply infidelity: Dragons mate for life and are faithful to a fault. But it does indicate that their genetic strains are long and very complex.

Western Dragons are a spectral delight. Much like their Eastern cousins, their color reflects their environmental needs and their diet. They are particularly adept at filtering minerals from their food and directing it into their scales. They can take lithium (red) from fish, iron (gold, green, and orange) from meat, potassium (lilac) and calcium (green) from vegetables, and so forth. Combine at will and you have a veritable spectrum of possibilities. While many Dragons have metallic highlights on

their ridge or tail, it is rare to find a solid gold, silver, or even bronze Dragon outside of fantasy fiction.

Fire and flight are two aspects of the Western Dragon which are found together in no other species. Fire, while flashy, is their defense of last resort. With claws, maws, and tails that can inflict serious damage, why waste their breath unless they have to? Spewing fire can also be destructive to their habitat, a concern they wish we humans had more frequently, especially in these drier, warmer times when field and forest can go up like tinder. Fire-breathing is also a highly skilled activity that, if done incorrectly, can leave Dragons vulnerable. While the exact process is not fully understood, cryptoherpetologists are almost 83 percent sure that Dragon fire is intricately connected to the combustion of volatile gases produced in pyronic sacs and ignited by flint powder sparking across hard plates at the back of the throat. These same gases are also essential for flight. Well-balanced fire can be coordinated with aerobatics, but long-term fire fights are usually land-based initiatives and can ground otherwise agile Dragons, putting them at a disadvantage. Though Westies will defend kith and kin with their last lick of flame and drop of blood, they tend to see self-sacrifice as a lack of

planning and imagination. Far better to keep their options open and stay mobile.

Mobility brings us to flight. How does such a massive creature get airborne, let alone stay that way? The secret lies in strong muscles and specialized bones. Though huge, Westies are relative lightweights, their skeletons made largely of hollow, or what are called pneumatic, bones. Paleontologists have made similar findings among certain dinosaurs (e.g., T. rex) and birds. The air cells in the bones provide strength without excessive weight. In conjunction with their flight-sacs—balloon-like structures analogous to a fish's swim bladder—Dragons are believed to direct residual fire gases through their honey-combed bones. In essence, their entire bodies get a lift and they are able to take to the skies with relative ease. They are marvels some would say fly in the face of the laws of nature and aerodynamics . . . but then, so are bumblebees . . . and 747s. Personally, I will take my chances with a Dragon.

Feathered Dragons

Scale the fog-shrouded Tepuis plateaus of the Guiana Highlands, explore the dense Amazonian wilderness, or spend New Year's Day wowed by Argentina's Iguazú Falls,

and you might just catch a fleeting glimpse of the last of the True Dragons: the Feathered or Southern Dragon— that is, if you're patient and very, very lucky.

Feathered Dragons are the smallest, rarest, and shyest gems of the draconic world. They are also the youngest. Birds grew from raptors, and Feathered Dragons developed from their more reptilian ancestors. As the climate changed and forests primeval pushed to the heavens, scales, even fine hairs, were not enough to keep them comfortable. Feathers were the next logical step on the evolutionary ladder. Feathers aided flight; flight took them into the tree tops. There they could roost and hunt, as their small size, serpentine necks, and prehensile tails gave them advantages over their larger kin.

At their height, long before they were revered by the Maya and the Fon, Feathered Dragons ranged from the primeval forests of Mexico to the fringes of Patagonia and throughout the lush jungles of ancient Africa, Madagascar, and southern India. They dwelt in the treetops, darting through the canopy, their rainbow plumage glistening in the tropical sun. Despite being surrounded by a bounty of delectable flora and fauna, this same environment kept them small, the better able to maneuver among trunks and branches, and vanish when they must.

TIP 2

✳

Dragon Watching

If you're inclined to Dragon watch, always remember and never forget:

- Know your season. Autumn is a time for courtship and coupling. You don't want to get in the way of Dragons in rut or traipse across mating grounds.
- Study up on lesser dragons in the region. As a group, they tend to be unpredictable; some are positively lethal.
- Distance is your friend, so take a camera with a good zoom lens.
- Stick to trails and designated lodgings.
- Pack in/Pack out. You are in the Dragons' home and should treat it accordingly.

Today, their habitat is restricted to the ever-shrinking rainforests of the New World. What drove them from the eastern hemisphere is a question that puzzles cryptoherpetologists to this day, with current theories revolving around climate change and an influx of European colonists exploiting the land and the people. No Feathered Dragon has been reported in sub-Saharan Africa since the nineteenth century, when Richard Burton and John Hanning Speke explored the continent's Great Lakes. This does not mean they're completely gone, of course; the forests of Africa are vast and deep, so the Dragons may have chosen to retreat. After all, they have done it before.

Unlike Western Dragons, who have been forced to adapt to leveled woods and urban sprawl, Feathered Dragons have chosen to remain far from people. The wildest of habitats are their playgrounds, and despite the advent of satellites and drones, they remain as elusive as smoke on a windy day. Even in the New World—in the now-ravaged heart of the Amazon—sightings are so infrequent that an accurate census is near impossible. The best scientific efforts are not helped by the fact that their shimmering acrobatics are often mistaken for close-knit flocks of macaws on the wing. Still, as long as the rainforests remain, we have reason to hope they do, too.

Facts and Figures

Though small by Dragon standards, never doubt for a second that our Feathered friends are formidable. Growing between 18 and 20 feet in length (much of which, as with Westies, is tail), they have wingspans reaching a spectacular 12 feet. Lean and reptilian, they tip the scales at a mere 300 pounds, true featherweights among Dragon species. Still, such mass can strain the treetops they call home. To keep from tumbling to the forest floor, they wrap their prehensile tails round trunks and sturdy limbs and distribute their weight safely among the branches.

Their bellies and legs are tightly scaled, lest they be vulnerable to attacks from below. The rest of their bodies are quilled. Fine bristle feathers to protect head and neck, downy under-plumage fit for nesting, a coat of contour plumes to keep them warm and dry, and sturdy flight feathers to carry them aloft. Though flight feathers are the most frequently shed, if found they are usually mistaken for the moltings of mundane species like harpy eagles or macaws. As long as this keeps the Dragon-curious away,

Feathereds are delighted to have eyes look elsewhere, especially when are dragonlets about.

Speaking of young ones, while Feathered Dragons are arboreal by nature and inclination, they nest exclusively in cliffside caves. A weyr can excavate an entire escarpment, honey-combing it with tunnels and dens, hatching hollows and pantry chambers, all for the security and comfort of the next generation.

When not nesting, the canopy is their playground. Unlike crepuscular Westies and Eastern Dragons, who enjoy the muted tones of dusk and dawn, Southern Dragons are most active in the full sun of day, when they can hunt and frolic, even vanish if need be, in the shifting forest shadows. Relentless omnivores, they dine on nuts, jaguar fruit, and pitajaya (dragon fruit); haul arapaima and catfish from the rivers; and pluck monkeys and boas from the trees. Like all Dragons, their senses are extremely acute, especially their eyesight. It is rumored they can spot a ripe cacao pod from a thousand yards or a school of pacu hiding in muddy flood waters.

Along with the usual defenses of tooth and claw that suffice for 99 percent of modern prey or foes, Feathered Dragons pack the most lethal venom in the world. In

large glands under their eye sockets, they concoct a complex hemorrhagic hemotoxin that flows through ducts along their upper jaw and out through retractable 8-inch fangs. This is a weapon of last resort, and we have no antidote for it. In fact, scientists have been trying to crack its composition for years with meager results. What they do know is that the venom is so potent that a drop will cause a rhino to bleed out in minutes. There may be no rhinos along the Rio Iguazú today, but Feathered Dragons were sure to have had run-ins with a variety of megafauna as recently as 12,000 years ago. Megatheres (giant sloths), elephant birds, cave lions, and half-ton bear dogs—there were some serious non-human dangers out there, as well as feasts waiting to be had. Cryptomythologists have hypothesized that the sanguinary results of envenomed Dragon bites contributed to the blood lore and rituals of pre-Columbian peoples. Despite the fact that such blood sacrifices were usually in the name of more humanistic deities such as Tlaloc and Itzamna, the theory remains sound. Given the premier place Feathered Dragons Sovereign Plumed Serpent and Quetzalcoatl hold as Creators in Mesoamerican cosmologies, it can be said that any blood gifted to the gods flows first for them.

A warning to anyone traveling through Feathered Dragons' forested domains: should you spy one of these iridescent beauties, keep your distance. And, no matter how inviting or abandoned they might seem, *never ever* explore their nesting caves. Though shy, they are Dragons, and all Dragons, even the most benevolent, are fiercely territorial.

Chapter Three

FROM EGG TO END: A DRAGON'S LIFE

Dragons are long-lived—barring lance or natural catastrophe, that is.

They start with fire and the crack of a shell and end—well, we're still not sure about that. In between, they have exciting, complex lives, full of fun, family, risk and reward—and no small measure of danger. While we know far more about Westies than Asian or Feathered Dragons, one thing is true of all: mating, nesting, hatching, and growing, each phase of a Dragon's existence is

in synch with Earth and sun, with days long and short, seasons wet and dry.

To understand a Dragon's life, it's best to begin at the beginning. While "Which came first, the Dragon or the egg?" is a question fit for a proper back-and-forth at the Cambridge Union, we will skip over it for now and go right to the first draconic peep.

A Dragon's life begins in late spring when the winds are warm and the world chartreuse with new growth. This is hatching season. After a year and a half ripening *in ovo*, nestlings are ready to put egg-tooth to shell and chip their way into the world ... none too soon for their brooding mother. For eighteen months she has tended her clutch, turning the eggs tenderly, adjusting their temperature with touch of scale and puff of breath. All that time, her devoted mate has kept her fed and amused. This can be an arduous task, and the extended family of the weyr lends a claw when they can, including short spells of egg-sitting so the mother can stretch her wings, go for a dip in the lake, and just take a break. Constructed out of boughs, loam, and heat-conducting minerals (the source of many a tale of golden hoards), it should be noted that a Dragon's nest is the perfect incubator. This is especially important in those cases when, through act of God or

man, a Queen finds herself alone in the world. A well-made nest allows her to keep her clutch warm enough to slip out for a quick feed without fear of temperature shock.

Seventy-three weeks into gestation, the little ones are all but mature. It's time for the Queen to move her brood from her secluded nesting chamber to the weyr's communal hatching ground. There, on a soft spread of clean branches and cushy gold, she places her eggs, one by one, and then resettles around them for the final two weeks of shell time. The eggs, soft and oval as a deflated beach ball when laid, are now round and ready to harden. In the final days, they begin to move and thrum, their tiny residents anxious to get out into the world. Mother Dragon responds with a gentle touch and soothing murmur.

Among Western Dragons, what happens next is nothing short of spectacular. In an act of parental love, Queen and Sire come together to gift the clutch with an incandescent blast of hatching fire. This serves two purposes: first, to push the Dragonlets into the final stage of pre-hatch development; and second, to heat the shells so that when they cool, they crackle and weaken enough to give the little ones a fighting chance at breaking free.

chapter three

55

> A Dragon's hatching day is full of ritual and splendor—after all, it's not every day that new Dragons come into the world.

A Dragon's hatching day is full of ritual and splendor—after all, it's not every day that new Dragons come into the world. Three days later, beneath the full Dragon Moon of May, excitement spreads through the weyr like Dragon fire. Kith and kin gather at the hatching ground and wait. Now it's up to Mom. When the moment is just right, she wraps herself in the aura of the Great Dragon, and from the depths of her maternal soul, lets loose the first soaring notes of her birthing anthem (*antienne eclorsion*). Note after divine note penetrates the shells, tickling the Dragonlets like a Quetzalcoatl feather. Then the Sire joins in, followed by the rest of the extended family until the entire weyr is rocking and rolling, including the eggs. They pitch back and forth, bumping against each other, expanding the flame cracks. The song stops. All that can be heard is the *chip-chip-chip* of egg teeth. For their first act of Dragon heroics, the little ones are busting out. Freedom is something they must claim for themselves.

Just out of the egg, Dragons are a scraggly lot, covered with egg residue and badly in need of a bath and a meal. Mother Dragon takes care of the former, showing them to the family pool or dust bowl for a good clean-up. Meanwhile, Father Dragon heads for the weyr larder to get their first feast: regurgitated meat and greens. Yum. This is his job now. In fact, for the first few weeks of their lives, he will be their primary caregiver. The rest of the enchantment will also chip in with teaching and tending. All claws on deck are a real asset, especially when the little ones get to their more rambunctious phases. Not that Mom won't be on hand, close to her children, strengthening the bond she began with them when nesting. But after eighteen months, she also needs to fly, hunt, and play, restoring herself to her full Dragonish glory. After all, she has years with her brood and needs to be the best Mother Dragon she can be.

A newborn Westie is roughly the size of a St. Bernard with small, velvety wings and tiny nubs on her brow eager to sprout into horns. Her long tail takes getting used to, tripping her this way and that as she tries to find her weyr-legs. After a couple of days tumbling about, inner Dragon grace will begin to emerge. Her scales are covered with a protective coat of fur she'll shed in a couple

of years. Of course, as form follows habitat, Polar Dragons keep a thick mane of fur into young adulthood—who can blame them?

Asian Dragons are perhaps the most like tiny versions of their grown-up selves. They pop out of the egg complete with manes and ankle tufts (skimpy though they may be), and fully functioning venom glands. They may not produce toxin in abundance, but what they do have is potent. Baby Feathered Dragons are also born packing lethal venom. Hatchlings are about the size of a grown macaw and covered with fine down that is replaced by brilliant plumage within their first year.

The first three years of a Dragon's life are a flurry of growth and activity. Weaned at about eight weeks of age, they enter their maiden summer with bright eyes, curious minds, and many lessons to learn—we're talking Survival 101.

Top of any survival list: eats. Dragons grow fast in their first few years, and understandably require a massive amount of food. It is essential for weanlings to be taught the ways of the woods, starting with meals that cannot run away: local flora. Despite their hardy constitutions, they need to learn which plants are good, which are sweet, which sour, and which will produce monstrous

bellyaches. While adults can and often do eat most any-thing, babies will be babies, and colicky Dragons are unhappy Dragons. There are also plants and fungi such as dream root, henbane, jimson weed, and myriad mush-rooms that in quantity are hallucinogenic. This is of par-ticular concern among the feathered beauties of South America. Many rainforest greens, fruits, and flowers pack a real wallop; young or old, a Dragon on a trip is not only a handful but a potential danger to herself and others. If taught well in the first year, such calamities can be avoided.

As far as prey goes, nothing teaches Dragonlets like play. With claws firmly on the ground, they are restricted to games of stalk-and-pounce as they perfect the ways of ambush predators while prowling the underbrush. Like cats, they chase and catch, release and catch again some hapless squirrel or woodchuck. They also learn to hunt as a pack, a most profitable means of snagging dinner when the grace and accuracy of flight are still months away.

Fishing is another skill Dragons master early, though when very young, they are more inclined to splash and play bobble stones than to patiently haunt the shallows while schools of sticklebacks tickle their toes. Of course,

chapter three

59

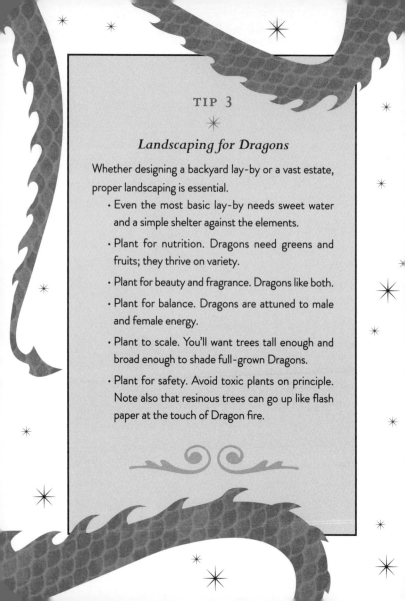

TIP 3

✳

Landscaping for Dragons

Whether designing a backyard lay-by or a vast estate, proper landscaping is essential.

- Even the most basic lay-by needs sweet water and a simple shelter against the elements.

- Plant for nutrition. Dragons need greens and fruits; they thrive on variety.

- Plant for beauty and fragrance. Dragons like both.

- Plant for balance. Dragons are attuned to male and female energy.

- Plant to scale. You'll want trees tall enough and broad enough to shade full-grown Dragons.

- Plant for safety. Avoid toxic plants on principle. Note also that resinous trees can go up like flash paper at the touch of Dragon fire.

a mawful of salmon or pike makes it all worthwhile in the end.

In their non-eating down-time, hatchlings let loose their natural curiosity and explore. They get to know the weyr's ins and outs and take part in the communal life. This includes some less-than-savory chores, like helping clean and refresh bedding. Being social creatures, Dragons, especially youngsters and juveniles, have a strict pecking order; spring hatchlings spend their first summer and autumn months finding their place in this hierarchy.

By year's end, Dragonlets have the basics of enchantment living well in hand, and not a moment too soon. A Dragon's second year is nothing short of incendiary, especially among Westies. Yearlings are big as grizzly bears and twice as fierce. Their permanent teeth are cut and sharpened, and their pyronic sacs are now fully functional. This way fire lies.

Before Dragons even think about breathing fire, they must first deal with changes in their physique, metabolism, and dietary cravings. Chests expand, making room for increased lung capacity. Body temperature rises, though by exactly how much we have yet to determine. (Even the most dedicated crypto vet will think twice before trying to take a Dragon's temperature.) And,

finally, mineral intake goes through the roof, specifically bits of chert, flint, and ore rich in phosphorus and iron. They are also likely to develop an interest in spicier vegetation such as ginger, goldmoss stonecrop, and the very hot tepin or turkey peppers. All this is in preparation—anticipation—of their first puff of flame. Any enchantment with youngsters will foresee these needs and have a store of fire stones and spicy treats at the ready.

Aside from learning their weyr's when-and-where fire rules—e.g., not near the woods, not during a drought—yearlings will be left more or less to their own devices. Practice makes perfect, and thanks to a natural fascination with flame and cinders, Dragons need very little encouragement to hone their skills. A word of warning: should you be hiking and come upon a charred rockhead or mirror-smooth sandpit, take a step back. These are the tell-tale signs of a fire-practice site, and depending on the season, there may well be young Dragons about. As always with Dragons in the wild, safety first.

Whether a by-product of their amped-up mineral need or simply an expression of their individuality, second-years also start to hoard. Shiny nuggets, river-tumbled stones, perhaps a bit of gear abandoned by a dracophobic camper or a festive banner from the local ranger sta-

tion; anything might strike their fancy and wind up as lair decor. Of course, their hoarding is restricted by the fact they're still earthbound. Once able to fly, the sky's the limit.

Year three is when the full draconic package comes together with two notable rites of passage: naming and flight.

Naming, more accurately the Remembrance of Names, is a soberly blissful occasion. It is believed that all enchantment names reside in the venerable depths of draconic history. When the time is right, in the company of family and friends, young Dragons mystically dip into this ancestral font and literally remember their names. From this moment on they are linked to the great *Familia Dracones*, and the entire weyr cheers.

Flight is both a little more straightforward and much more wow-inducing. In the summer of their third year, Dragons are finally strong enough, their wings big enough, to take to the skies. Time at last to set aside gawky Dragonlet ways. This doesn't happen all at once, of course. In spring, the soft velvet that covered their wings since birth sloughs off. This is nothing short of a draconic metamorphosis. Rubbing and burnishing until the last bit of fuzziness is gone, they now sport splendid pairs of

smooth, leathery sails. Free from their casing, these new wings grow at an alarming rate, reaching proportionate size before midsummer. This is hardly a time for idleness, though. To prepare for the big day, Dragons spend hours strengthening their flight muscles, getting used to the feel of wing-vanes billowing in the wind. They also start to tinker with their fire breathing, learning how to balance flame with gas-filled flight sacs. Parents and elders are basically observers during this time, letting nature teach as only nature can.

At the height of midsummer, the three-year olds tramp en masse to the top of the nearest bluff. (Weyrs are often located on cliffs for just this purpose, as well as the obvious advantage of high ground.) Nostrils flaring in the breeze, they spread their wings and step off. Though this first flight will be only an easy glide on thermal updrafts, it is intoxicating enough to encourage them to try again ... and again ... and again. Having little else to do besides eat, grow, and perfect their dragonish ways, by the end of their fourth year Westies are such pros on the wing as to make even Bessie Coleman jealous. They will swoop and dive, plucking hare from field and trout from stream, not to mention putting a shine on their skills with aerial Dragon fire. Flight also broadens a young Dragon's

TIP 4

Calling Dragons

Build a lay-by and Dragons will come. Eventually. Some people believe they can speed up the process with a summoning. An open heart and Dragon empathy never hurt. And patience.

Find a quiet spot where you feel connected to the elements. Breathe deep, clear your mind of human clutter, and reach out with your mind's eye. Envision a Dragon—or two, don't be greedy—swooping out of the sky to the safe place you've created for her. The place where she can be herself. Repeat your call at dusk and dawn (active times for Dragons), weaving your welcome layer upon layer, day after day. The more regular the ritual, the more efficacious for you both.

horizons. Earth and heavens are now theirs to explore, including supervised visits to neighboring weyrs. With the prospect of mating mere decades away, it's never too early to make friends across bloodlines.

You may have noticed that I have been speaking mostly about European Dragons.

Why is that? The truth is, Asian Dragon isolation and Feathered Dragon rarity have left major holes in our knowledge base. We do know that Feathered Dragons are early flyers. They tumble from their lofty burrows and skim through the rainforest canopy at the beginning of their second year. As with most things Dragon, this is assumed to be an adaptation to their environment. If they're born in a cliffside den, it's nearly impossible for them to get out and learn draconic essentials without being able to fly.

When it comes to flight and Asian Dragons, they are, quite simply, a puzzlement. We know that some of them don't fly at all. Earth and Mountain Dragons seem to be content to live their lives with feet on the ground. As for those who do play among the clouds, how they manage without wings is a mystery. Cryptoherpetologists who have been privileged to study these extraordinary beings insist it is a matter more metaphysical than physi-

cal, a report that leaves us with many questions and few answers. They've also discovered that those who do fly don't get airborne until their ninth year. (The number nine is very auspicious in Eastern Dragon circles.)

Adolescence is a long and tumultuous time for Dragons. Between youth and sexual maturity, they have decades of growth, hormones, and discovering their individual inner Dragon. This is when they break free of their clutchmates and come into their own as a grown member of the weyr. The latter includes taking a more active role in the care and education of the next generation. This creates a fair division of labor within the community (adult Dragons welcome any down time they can get when there are fledglings around) and injects the juveniles with a real boost of self-confidence. They are the big brothers, sisters, and cousins now, with stories of their own to tell and wisdom—limited though it may be—to pass along.

Of course, all work (even the rewarding kind) makes for very cantankerous Dragons. And at this stage, hormonal juveniles have literally have energy to burn. Without release, tensions rise, tempers flare, and injuries (usually unintended) can happen. Like people and other complicated species, Dragons turn to play. Once used

to improve their basic hunt, fire, and flight skills, games are now used to prevent all-out inter-enchantment tussles. On land, water, or in the air, adolescents will spend a third of their waking hours playing Gargoyles, Bauble Hunt, and Gryphons, Elves, & Wizards. Besides wearing them out, these activities strengthen bonds and can bring even the most introverted Dragon out of her shell, all skills that are essential to the weyr's survival.

Adulthood means choosing partners, and Dragons' choices are life-long, personal, and diverse. Instinctively aware of genetic strengths, weakness, and the rules that govern both, Queens and Sires from the same weyr are forbidden to mate. This is why adolescent travels and long-distance attachments are so important. Extra-weyr connections made in youth can blossom into life-long relationships. Some Dragons partner up with no intention of breeding, and they're naturally not bound by the same proscriptions. Still others choose a solitary life, preferring to remain "attached" to the community as a whole rather than an individual. Weyrs are ever mindful of population control, so such choices are welcomed without question. They also provide a ready supply of "aunts" and "uncles" able to dragon-sit when needed.

Depending on the species, female Dragons become sexually mature at the ripe young (for Dragons) age of between thirty-five and fifty. Males, always a little slower, take another decade or so to reach adulthood and, almost as importantly, to gain the emotional maturity necessary to be a Sire. Being a Dragon is difficult enough; they don't need the complication of callow parenting. A Queen can lay once in a generation. This may seem like an eternity to us, but given draconic longevity—and the need not to have too many little maws to feed at once—it serves enchantments perfectly.

Courtship is a long-term affair. Beginning innocently enough with fledgling play dates, over years of getting to know one another, fun-fellows can become comrades, comrades confidants, and confidants mates. (All this gives a whole new meaning to games of Catch the Dragon's Tail.)

Depending on the female/male ratio in any given environment, more than one budding Sire might set his sights on a young Queen. When Dragons ruled the Earth in the distant past, such situations were resolved with fierce battles, often to the death. However, when the Dark Times came upon them, things changed: slayers were around every corner and crag; Dragons saw no point in doing their job for them. So it was that battles for a Queen's paw became the ritualized contests of skill with wing and fire we see today. Of course, Dragon mating is more than just chest-thumping and hormones. No matter who is victorious, the Queen always has the final say. If all goes well, disparate weyrs will come together beneath the Harvest Moon to secure the peace and consecrate a joyful union.

Bright and shiny after their late-summer molt, Dragons enter the clear, crisp days of autumn eager to mate. No matter how long a pair has been together, if the Queen's in season, it always feels like the very first time. Over the next few weeks, gifts large and small are exchanged, dens tidied, and nests woven. The air becomes thick with pheromones, all spice and floral. Then the Queen takes the cast skin from her tail spade, mixes it with herbs, amber, honey, and horn bits, and tumbles it into a passion ball—a powerful aphrodisiac she sets aside until just the right moment when she shares it with her mate.

Try though they might, even the most dedicated cryptoherpetologists are still in the dark when it comes to actual Dragon mating . . . and that is as it should be. What we do know is that after the autumnal equinox, a breed-

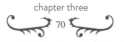

ing pair's behavior (and indeed the entire enchantment's behavior) changes. There are only six weeks between conception and egg-laying, barely the blink of an eye in Dragon time, and much to do. Most notably, the Queen's appetite increases—a lot. She is now eating for as many as a half-dozen or more, not to mention the extra nutritional demands of shell-forming. Most notably, massive amounts of calcium and protein are essential; even if she's the best hunter in the weyr, she'll need help meeting her needs. This is where family comes in, bringing home an extra deer or fish or stocking the enchantment stores with late-season greens. Additional helpings of feldspar or dolomite help immensely, and coastal Dragons have been known to chow down on mouthfuls of shells. The change in diet shows itself in her scales, giving a gravid Queen a deep coppery sheen, a sure sign that mating was successful and a new generation is on its way.

The proud papa-to-be spends his spare time collecting extras for their nesting chamber. Of course, the quest for the perfect nest can require trips far from home. While away, he is comforted by the fact that his Queen will be surrounded by a weyr full of solicitous kin (all the more reason for the intricate social life of Dragons.) Bits and pieces collected, Sire and Queen set about refining, at times even

totally rebuilding, their already-substantial nest until it is perfect.

In frosty November, the pair retreat to the nesting chamber warmed with Dragon fire, and the Queen lays her eggs.

Thus, the cycle begun decades before, begins again.

It is safe to say that by the time Dragons hit their seventy-fifth year, their routines are more or less set. A Queen will have seen one clutch grow to maturity, perhaps have another ready to leave the nest. In between, she and her mate help raise others in the weyr and fight the creep of ennui. Thank the Great Dragon for draconic curiosity and their rich social life, without which Dragons would surely be bored silly. And bored Dragons, like bored people, tend to be troublesome. So, they fly thousands of miles, spin hundreds of yarns, and dine and dance beneath myriad full moons. This is the pattern of their adult years, but just how long does this keep going on?

That, of course, depends on species and good fortune, though even the shortest-lived Dragons can hope to see 300 hatching-day celebrations. If anecdotal evidence is accurate (and when it comes from the Dragon's mouth, it usually is) there are elders in the world today who listened to Henry Purcell play the organ in Westminster Abbey and flew escort for Queen Christina as she went into exile; who saw the last stones set in the Taj Mahal and guarded Bashō as he wandered the backroads of Honshu. This surpasses the outer limits of human mortality so greatly as to seem positively fantastic. And perhaps it is. Those in the budding field of cryptogerontology (and their children for generations to come) have the task of finding truth among tales and improving our understanding of long-in-the-tooth Dragons as best they can.

So, what *do* we know? When Dragons enter their fourth century, their scales grow brittle and lose some of their luster. Among Eastern Dragons, whiskers and ankle tufts turn white as the first snow on Tian Shan. The old ones are more vulnerable to the elements and the rare illnesses their younger kin shake off with ease. They also begin to slow down. Spur-of-the-moment flights to visit distant relatives are less enticing than stories and games with the

So comes snow after fire, and even dragons have their endings.
—J.R.R. Tolkien,
The Hobbit

great-great-great-granddragonlets. And they are always welcome, honored as receptacles of wisdom and keepers of the draconic flame.

J.R.R. Tolkien knew well that "[s]o comes snow after fire, and even dragons have their endings" (Tolkien, 1970). Still, the big question remains: What happens when these ancient Dragons die? We certainly have records of violent passings where the earth was burnt bare by caustic Dragon blood. But what happens after a long and fruitful life when the days simply wind down, as they must? Here is where lore proves better than science and a story is as true as a dozen hard facts. Perhaps they return to the mists of the Otherworld or crumble to dust under the weight of all their years.

My favorite *fabulae dracones mori* is one of the most ancient. It tells of an island in the Sacred Sea. On the island stands a great gnarled rowan tree, tall as a sequoia and older than time. Its roots dig deep into the rocky soil; its branches like fingers reach up into the clouds. And round the tree sleep six golden Dragons, guardians of the Sacred Way. When a Dragon's wings grow heavy and mortality screams through muscle and bone, she summons the last of her strength and makes her way to this Isle of the Six. The guardians welcome her with fiery elegy and

thunderous clatter of scales. They weave a song of Dragon passions and deeds, of centuries lived and generations born, raised, and left behind, of the thousand-thousand Dragons who came before. And, as the last note fades, they send her up, through argent rowan boughs, into the embrace of the Great Dragon.

Sir Terry Pratchett wrote, "No one is actually dead until the ripples they cause in the world die away" (Pratchett, *Reaper Man*, 1991). With the passing of Dragons, the mountains tremble and the heavens weep. The Universe feels their absence like an aching wound. Their ripples radiate on and on through ages only imagined.

In their wake lies an ancient truth: Dragons are too wondrous, too rare, to ever truly die.

Chapter Four

DRAGON SPECIES SMALL

Are you the sort of dracophile for whom size doesn't matter? Are you intrigued by the odd and exotic and eager to explore remote environs? Then you are sure to be a fan of the pseudo, or lesser, dragons of the world. Guivres and musussus, ropen and gowrows, are as distinct as their habitats and the people who share them. They range in size from wyverns and fire drakes nearly as large as proper Western Dragons to harpy-esque tree-skimmers and whimsical žaltys who can hide beneath a rhubarb plant. Though True Dragons take our breath

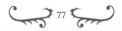

away, it is often these lesser dragons living in our midst, from the familiar (dare I say "common") to the unique, who remind us of draconic wonder on a daily basis.

One of the marvelous things about Dragon Studies is how generation after generation, we continue to discover new things and push the empirical and theoretical envelopes. This has been particularly true when it comes to lesser dragons and their place in the greater draconic family. These strange, quasi-reptilian creatures have always been classified as distaff offshoots of the Big Three, their external characteristics providing broad hints at shared kinship. Yet it is only recently that cryptogeneticists have been able to trace their familial connections with something approaching a scientific certainty, making connections we cannot help but celebrate. Pseudodragons are not just dragons in name, but dragons in blood, too.

Hyperbole aside, "So many dragons, so little time," are words to live by when it comes to lesser species. Since dracophiles tend to be most captivated by dragons they might actually encounter in field, stream, or garden, these are the species on which we'll focus. Hydras, for example, may be fascinating, but they're virtually extinct these days. In these pages I'll also throw in a few of my personal favorites for good measure. As for the rest,

they're not being ignored, simply left for the more academically minded.

A word of warning: Just because pseudodragons are smaller and generally less intimidating than True Dragons, do not assume they are safer or take them for granted. They are wild, willful, and well-equipped to defend themselves. Most of them prefer retreat to confrontation, but any frightened or cornered dragon should be considered dangerous.

Lake Dragons & Sea Serpents

No stranger to the rare and unusual, director Werner Herzog once opined, "What would an ocean be without a monster lurking in the dark? It would be like sleep without dreams." I like to think our aquatic friends would agree.

Ponds flow into lakes, lakes into rivers, and ultimately, rivers into seas. Water, water everywhere, rife with dragons of all sorts, sizes, and dispositions. Pint-sized kiau bless the streams and ponds of Asia, leviathans of the deep confound

> What would an ocean be without a monster lurking in the dark? It would be like sleep without dreams.
> —Werner Herzog

submariners, and their freshwater cousins who long ago went upriver and made their homes in the great inland lakes attract the curious and skeptical alike. Most are unsung residents of the deep, yet a handful of them have made real names for themselves: Champs, Nessie, Ogopogo, the Lake Labynkyr Devil (a surly Siberian creature who has by all accounts earned his epithet). Even Noah Webster included one of their kind in the 1828 edition of his dictionary:

> SEA-DRAGON, n. [sea and dragon.] A marine monster caught in England in 1749, resembling in some degree an alligator, but having two large fins which served for swimming or flying. It had two legs terminating in hoofs, like those of an ass. Its body was covered with impenetrable scales, and it had five rows of teeth. (*American Dictionary of the English Language*, 1828)

Though water dragons are found around the world, from tropical pools to temperate marshlands, Yule-iced lakes to desert wadis, they are almost all distant relations of the great Eastern Dragons. Less complex and intelligent than their genetic foredragons, to be sure, but the link is

unmistakable to even the most casual observer. They share the same long, wingless physiques, perfect for surfing breakers and rippling through shoal and sound; the same wide eyes and tactile whiskers. They also fill a similar niche in the ecosystem. Because rivers, lakes, and seas are lifelines for humanity, water dragons—especially the small, approachable species—are considered guardians of the waves, briny and sweet. Vegetarian kiaus, for example, will clear out invasive plants, like water hyacinth or alligator weed, and unclog the streams so indigenous swimmers and waterfowl can breathe free and thrive. Their presence is indicative of healthy waters and abundant fishing. Is it any wonder that, like their Eastern Dragon kindred, kiaus inspire the reverence of the two-legs in their neighborhood . . . even if they do tangle lines or rip the occasional net?

Easily half of the catalogued pseudodragon species consider water or wetlands their home. Yet despite their numbers and distribution, their cautious natures and unexplored or inaccessible environs make sightings rare. This is particularly true of the deep-sea Dragons like the ryu-jin of the western Pacific. Named after the cosmic King of Japanese Dragons, there have not been more than a dozen ryu-jin sightings in the last fifty years. Nonbelievers are of course quick with a cynical retort: "See? They're just legends!"

But as any marine biologist will tell you, even with state-of-the-art submersibles and undersea drones, the ocean is just too vast and too littered with myriad hidey-holes for beings large and small. To a lesser extent, the same can be said of Loch Ness. Deep and crevassed, with a passage to the North Sea, the loch is the perfect habitat for a reclusive lake dragon. With a little belief and a lot of patience, you never know who you'll see rising through the morning haze.

To maximize their chances for survival, many water dragons follow the seasons and currents between salt water and fresh. This is especially true of those who summer north (or south) of the 50th parallel. When the winds turn cold and the lakes begin to ice around their edges, small water dragons may hibernate in the mud, but the large ones have other plans. They follow the currents to warmer climes and plentiful feeding. The January waters off the Canary Islands or the Baja Peninsula, for example, are alive with dragons stuffing themselves silly on elvers and sardines. There they renew acquaintances and court and spark in anticipation of a fertile spring. Though cryptoherpetologists are just beginning to see the effect of rising sea levels and growing oceanic dead zones on these remarkable creatures, as with all things climate-change related, the long-term prognosis is worrisome, to say the least.

Caveats given, if you want to go dragon-watching, you could do worse than wandering remote coastlines on a cool misty morning. Check for tell-tale signs, like belly-trails through the dunes or paw prints of draconian size along the shore. Then wait. For it is in water dragon nature to play among the forests of reed and kelp, disguise themselves as moss-caped boulders, and tickle puffin toes with their whiskers.

And remember that as much as we may be seeking a glimpse of Champs or a school of Mekong kiaus, they couldn't care less about our quest. Their lives have their own rhythms and secret joys. And in light of shabby human treatment in the past, many dragons prefer to stay hidden. Can you blame them? Still, they are there all the same, for those who can see them. And safe is always better than seen.

Wyverns and Fire Drakes

Where water dragons' sinuous Eastern Dragon ancestry is emblazoned across their broad scaly shoulders, wyverns

and fire drakes turn to the west and wear their claims to distant Western Dragon heritage with pride.

It is hardly hyperbolic to say that the most conspicuous dragons in recent years are Drogon, Rhaegar, and Viserion in the television series *Game of Thrones,* an adaptation of George R. R. Martin's *A Song of Ice and Fire* fantasy books. Credit to Mr. Martin and the wizards of special effects: these magnificent CGI creatures have grown through the seasons into fire-breathers of enormous size, strength, and loyalty. What riveted dracophile hasn't shared Tyrion's childhood plea for their own dragon—"It wouldn't even have to be a big dragon ... it could be a small one like me"—or wept at the thought of their extinction (Martin and Benioff, 2016)? And when they take wing, who watching doesn't get a visceral thrill and wish they, like Daenerys Targaryen, were riding astride Drogon, incinerating enemies with flair? Now, while they may be True Dragons in Westeros, any cryptoherpetologist who can count will tell you that on Earth, they are actually wyverns. Two legs, two wings—a dead giveaway.

I do not fault the popular imagination for this wyvern/Dragon blunder; humans have been making it for centuries, particularly in the arts, where creative license often sides with symbolism over zoological accuracy. One place

they've received the distinction they deserve—and the requisite number of limbs—is in heraldry. Indicative of their abundance in the world, they're the most common draconic symbol on crest and shield. While sharing some of the same heraldic traits with True Dragons—such as strength, valor, guardianship, and excellent eyesight—they are, in the end, pale versions of Westies. Nobles may claim wyverns for their coats of arms, but Dragons remain for royalty or nations.

With a range extending from Europe to the Siberian hinterlands, wyverns are the largest lesser dragons to sport wings. Averaging 18 to 20 feet from tip to tail, they are easily distinguished from the local Westies by their conspicuous lack of front legs. Their forelimbs are batlike wings with heavily scaled carpal joints (wrists) on which they can walk when needed, and from which emerge elongated phalanges tipped with lethal claws for grasping and rending prey. They are almost exclusively carnivorous, a fact some believe contributes to their fierce dispositions, and in turn, their bad reputations and lethal wyvern-human conflicts.

In the wild, wyverns have been known to hobnob with Western enchantments, and, at a distance or on the wing, can be taken for juvenile Westies, especially if fire

is involved. Conversely, Dragons have been mistaken for wyverns with dire results: blamed for herd raids, barn razings, and otherwise unruly acts. This, combined with the growing anti-Dragon sentiments of the Common Era, led to centuries of tension and bloodshed on all fronts. Needless to say, such confusion and general muddying of the draconic narrative continues to this day. How many victims of knight or saint were not True Dragons but much smaller and more vulnerable wyverns? It's anyone's guess, though if the paintings of the day are any indication, very few of these heroes—Sts. George and Michael included—faced actual Dragons.

Hike the rocky uplands of Europe at twilight and look to the horizon. There, if you are lucky, you'll see draconic forms perched in silhouette on tor and crag, singing to the moonrise. These are fire drakes, who, like wyverns, are frequently mistaken for Western Dragons. If one doesn't look too closely, that is ... especially around the shoulders.

Drakes are heavy-bodied, reptilian quadrupeds who long ago opted for ground living rather than soaring through the air or plunging beneath the waves. They can grow to approximately 30 feet in length (much of which is tail) and look very much like over-fed Westies sans wings. Unlike

other terrestrial dragons, drakes are not classified as diggers, preferring instead to take up residence in existing caves, grottos, and abandoned mines. This often puts them in proximity to and conflict with humans. Flocks and herds roaming the moorlands unattended are a temptation few drakes (or indeed *any* Dragon with a healthy appetite) can ignore. Subsequent clashes are similar to the recent wolf-farmer conflicts near Yellowstone National Park, though wolves are infinitely more fragile than dragons, especially against modern weaponry.

It's not that drakes go looking for tussles; slow and lumbering by draconic standards, with stolid temperaments, they prefer strategic retreats to savage encounters. Backs to their caves, they will bellow and bluff, puffing themselves up and flashing their neck furls. A sentiment shared by all save the wildest dragons is that a proper scare is as good as a battle any day. But don't assume they are safe. Pursued into their lair, they will stand their ground with the best of them, driving

Drakes ... can grow to approximately 30 feet in length.

intruders away with licks of red-hot flame. They are called fire drakes, after all.

Skimmers and Diggers

Smaller, lesser known, and so diverse that at times, they're hardly recognizable as dragons, tree skimmers and diggers were once found on every continent, including Antarctica. Their range is more restricted today (a sorry truth for all draconic creatures), but they are still here when many species have gone extinct. That they remain so numerous and worldly, so likely to cross our paths, attests to their remarkable adaptability.

Look up from hedgerow to treetop, country gable to penthouse eave, and you just might find a skimmer drowsing in the sun. Lithe and graceful, with playful curiosities, skimmers are believed to share their lineage with Feathered Dragons, though they lack plumage—that's a trait reserved for their capital-D cousins. However, their haunts and habits are similar enough to convince even the most skeptical cryptoherpetologists of the shared, if distant, kinship.

Regal as eagles and small as horned chameleons, skimmers are a wonder of diversity. Some are full-winged, flapping their way through their sphere with precise dexterity. Others glide like colugos (flying lemurs) or sugar gliders on great sails of thin skin running along their flanks. Recently, cryptoherpetologists have added a third group to the lot: draconic climber/leapers who have neck furls that umbrella open to catch the air and give them extra lift. All have coloration that helps them merge with their surroundings, and all nest aloft so they can live their lives from egg hatch to final breath without setting claw to ground.

Whether flapping, gliding, or leaping, even the biggest skimmers travel as silently as owls. With stealth and cunning, they swoop and dive from above, taking their meals on the fly and sending intruders scurrying for the hills. Like Feathered Dragons, the skimmer habitat makes fire an unworkable defense. Most rely on simple fang and claw and the element of surprise, though some, like the iaculus of the Mediterranean, have a wicked venom-laced bite that will fell creatures ten times their size. If you are in their neighborhood, watch out. They are ambush predators who do not hesitate hurling themselves from on high and sinking their fangs deep into the necks of their prey. [Note: Cryptozoologists have not gotten up close with all tree skimmers and warn that given their dietary requirements, it is likely that the smallest of them are also venomous. Be careful. They may look like harmless little reptiles, but they're not.]

Humans have been clearing woodlands for farming for centuries, but it wasn't until the start of the industrial age that we began absolutely decimating the world's forests. As with Feathered Dragons, deforestation endangers tree skimmers large and small. And as their survival instincts kick in, those skimmers who can have made their way to alternative vertical environments: cities.

In the high-rise nooks and crannies among cathedral arches and bridge towers, urbanized skimmers build nests and dip and dive for fun and food. This puts a whole new twist on Tolkien's admonition: "It does not do to leave a live dragon out of your calculations if you live near him" (Tolkien, *The Hobbit*, 1970). Fortunately for one and all, metropolitan landscapes are full of prey and unexpected forage. In their new steel and glass wilderness, dragons trade off-the-branch papaya and cacao pods for pilfered rooftop-garden fare, and marmoset and vine snake for pigeon, squirrel, and rat. Invaluable as this makes them when it comes to pest control, it is important to remember that skimmers are opportunistic feeders and thus not always as discriminating as we might wish. In lean times and hatching season they have been known to drop out of the blue and abscond with small family pets. Dog parks are especially vulnerable for their varied and plentiful

"menu." Some cities have taken to fitting their parks with skimmer alarms, which have met with limited success. While they work very well for visiting birds of prey, most dragons find the ruckus more amusing than frightening and have been known to set them off for the sheer fun of it. If skimmers have moved into your neighborhood, keep your eyes on the skies and never leave your cats or dogs, guinea pigs, rabbits, or tea-cup pigs unattended.

In the spirit of falconers of old, a handful of dracophiles have tried "taming" citified tree skimmers with nesting boxes, feeding stations, and patience. Intriguing as this sounds, in the interest of shared safety, WAFDE (World Association for Dragons Everywhere) discourages this practice. While they surely appreciate shelter and nosh, all accounts have it that the dragons insist on retaining their wildness. Dragons will be dragons, after all. The important lesson here is that dragons will not hesitate to respond with tooth and claw if they feel threatened even in urbanized settings and even by a human they've known for months. If taming experiments go awry and a skimmer problem arises, contact your nearest cryptoherpetologist or WAFDE representative immediately. Better yet, don't mess with their natural ways in the first place.

TIP 5

Dragons and Others

Having a Dragon in the family is exhilarating, but some proper precautions must be taken.

- Make sure insurance policies—particularly fire and medical—are ample, premiums paid in full.

- All introductions should be made in the presence of a responsible Dragon Keeper; if hatchlings are involved, at least one *parente draconis*.

- Get Dragons and children used to each other when young ... and curious, fearless, and eager to make friends.

- Dragons like most companion animals, especially cats, chinchillas, and smaller breeds of goat.

- Keep emergency numbers (e.g., the vet) on speed dial, just in case.

Chilean copperbacks, Yowah growlers, Highland Beithir —diggers are as colorful as the rare gems and minerals they shake from their scales. As their name implies, diggers are terrestrial dragons. Their ancestry is murkier than that of other pseudodragons, though experts are leaning toward them being a hybrid offshoot of proto-Eastern and Western Dragons combined. When the rains turned sour and fire lit up the skies, they were perfectly equipped to burrow, shelter, and greet the dawn of another millennium. Today they make their mark in arid and semi-arid regions considered inhospitable to many species. By living mostly underground, they are able to survive intense heat as well as find water and food where others can't.

Slung low to the ground with powerful legs and claws, as well as hard beaklike snouts that can chip through hillsides with ease, diggers are frequently mistaken for large savannah monitors, giant thorny devils, or mutant armadillo lizards. Misidentification can be extremely hazardous for the casual hiker or spelunker with an undiscerning eye. Good-sized monitors, for example, can deliver bone-crushing bites with sharp, venom-laced teeth. While certainly painful, unless you tangle with Komodo monitors (dragons only in the vernacular, though that

is obviously a misnomer), who have both venom and mouthfuls of antibiotic-immune bacteria, you'll very likely survive. The same cannot be said of encounters with digger dragons. All diggers are not only considerably larger than mundane reptiles, but they also have lethal defenses, including venomous quills, heel spurs, and tail barbs. Trust me—they will not hesitate to use them.

Though diggers seldom compete with other Dragons for creature comforts, they have found themselves increasingly at odds with humans intent on exploiting their environs and the riches they contain. But this is nothing new: in the Stone Age, miners tracked diggers into tunnels littered with valuable ores and precious stones, not that the dragons cared a twitch about such things. Those precious minerals were simply the byproduct of travels and lairkeeping. To humans, however, they were a means to status and power. And they looked nice, something capital-D Dragons certainly appreciate. (They do *love* sparklies.) In the early days, simple spears proved no match for dragon bite and scale, so our ancestors contented themselves with rummaging through abandoned tunnels, gleaning flakes and nuggets left behind. The result was an almost symbiotic relationship between human and dragon.

As the Stone Age turned Bronze, the once mutually benign relationship turned sour. As human settlements and villages grew, so too did human greed and weaponry, often made from the very metals found in dragon tunnels. Unable to take wing or dive beneath the waves, diggers were left standing their ground, a posture of necessity. From the Urals and Andes to the deserts of Africa and Australia, they made humans rich and got little save pain in return. Over time, this made them among the most aggressive pseudodragons in the world.

Today, diggers no longer deflect the occasional spear or arrow but must contend with explosives and gigantic earth-movers ripping through their habitats. Sadly, the largest of their kind are no longer with us, unable to survive the onslaught to hide and home. Some of the smaller species, like the Tyr druics of southwest England, are not only here but, by recent accounts, are making a comeback. As we've abandoned mines hither and yon, they've uttered gleeful yawps and reclaimed their ancestral abodes.

If, in your travels, you cross paths with a digger, give it a wide berth. They may be protected species now, but they have long memories. They will defend kith and kin, and even the smallest of them can send you to the hospital with a chomp.

Dragon Keeper's Choice and Something New

Every dracophile I know has their favorites among the lesser dragons. How could they not? Personally, I have a soft spot for the smallest, most capricious of the pseudos: *Draco domesticus*, aka house dragons.

Long, long ago, pint-sized Neolithic pseudodragons found something endearing about walls and roofs and the humans who kept them. Go figure. While most of their bigger kin remained hidden, eyes shining in the dark, these little ones were courageous and curious. They ventured forth, into the umbra of our fires. Some didn't like what they found, retreating back into the shadows. But some stayed. We gave them food and a place by the hearth, and they, in turn, rewarded us with blessings, shiny objects (house dragons are the magpies among the pseudos), and their protection. From the paperbark gunyahs of the Australian outback to the frosty earth lodges of the northern tundra, from Latvian cottages to Bengali bungalows, their story, out of those ancient embers, grew intricately linked with ours.

House Dragons (HDs) are often considered miniature versions of the True Dragons in the region, which has led some to refer to them as dainty or cute. Let me be very clear: just because these dragons are small(ish)—usually under three feet in length—does not mean they're "cute." Cute dragons are the product of toy makers and cartoon animators. In the real world, Dragons True and pseudo- are beautiful and frightening, grotesque and awesome, and yes, adorable just out of the egg in a way that only a Queen mother could appreciate. But they are *not* cute. Even house dragons.

Fferm gwybers, smij, nauis, gnar nagas, tangaroas . . . with names as varied as their forms and idiosyncrasies, practically every corner of the world and every culture has its house dragon. They fly and slink, have fiery tails and nubbin horns, and colors as radiant as habitat and diet allow. Pisuhänds build nests of scraps, socks, and straw, and aitvaras are especially fond of herb omelettes. As our homes and gardens became theirs, they'd guard them and us with fierce territoriality. HDs also have a special fondness for children, and chil- dren generally reciprocate. (As Rachel Carson remarked in *The Sense of Wonder*, "Many children . . . delight in the small and inconspicuous" [Carson, 1998].) I like to believe this shared affinity comes from the fact that children do not

doubt their existence the way some adults do. Either way, kids and house dragons go perfectly together; you couldn't ask for better or more diligent babysitters. Whether in the playroom or the back garden, the dragons are sure to infuse their duties with a sense of fun. Many a tale of spooks in the night and puckish sprites are actually contorted tales of a local žaltys or smij on patrol, which surely makes them smile.

Whether those first house dragons latched onto the dwellings or the people in them is still not settled science. That they followed nomadic tribes of yore leads one to believe they're partial to us mere mortals. When we moved, they moved. This fact is also borne out in our more recent exoduses. The wars, famines, and natural disasters of the nineteenth and twentieth centuries have displaced millions from Europe, Asia, and now the Middle East. And when they came to new shores, with memories past and futures uncertain, their dragons came with them.

> Kids and house dragons go perfectly together; you couldn't ask for better, more diligent, babysitters.

Whatever land embraced these new souls embraced new house dragons, too—even if they didn't know it.

The New World has become a particular haven for HDs from all corners of the globe. The newcomers have mingled with indigenous species from the Yucatán to the Pacific Northwest. This can cause problems, especially in urban areas where space is at a premium. Like most creatures, including humans, dragons unfamiliar with each other may be standoffish or even snappish at first. Add to this being protective of their home and people, and dust-ups will occur; it's just a fact of house-dragon life. Proper introductions and a full pantry go a long way toward ironing out rough spots. Remember that, while gifting is in a house dragon's blood, their concept of who owns what can be fuzzy at the best of times. Establish firm rules about pilfered goods and gaudies. This will prevent scuffles, hurt feelings, even litigation, down the line.

Some dracophiles think of house dragons as gateway companions for would-be Dragon keepers; with diligence and care, they can be. Get to know the species in your neighborhood. Confuse a gentle zitny smij with a semi-social tree skimmer, and you're apt to pay a visit to the ER. Learn their needs and habits. After all, you wouldn't expect an eagle to be drawn to a hummingbird

feeder. And definitely learn the local laws. In Lithuania, for example, all people with an aitvaras in their home must register with the authorities. This practice hearkens back to the fourteenth century, when there was a nasty clash between dragons and church, something that does not bear repeating. Of course, in the end, all the papers and licenses in the world do not mean ownership. Like their True kin, house dragons come and go as they please.

It should be noted that unlike virtually all other pseudo- species, house dragons have an acute sense of right and wrong. You might even say they are moralistic … or at least situationally so. If a house dragon's people are generous and kind to friends and strangers, two-legs and four-legs alike, they will reap the blessings of dragon and Goddess for generations. If, however, the hearts of a house turn cold and mean, then guardian dragons will depart without so much as a glance over their tails. They will take with them all treasure and goodwill, and none of their kind will grace that threshold until lessons are learned and changes are made. Don't expect a quick turn-around: house dragons will not be conned by half-hearted shows of kindness; they have been known to abandon a family and their descendants forever if not convinced of proper growth, contrition, and respect. They're hard

taskmasters for sure, but their company is well worth the effort.

With human populations exploding, wilderness vanishing, and climate change wreaking havoc from pole to pole, it is a tragic truth that extinction levels are on the rise among creatures both crypto and mundane. In this environment, when a species beats the odds, it is cause for celebration. When, in a remote corner of the globe, a new species is discovered, it is an absolute miracle. I want to conclude this chapter by talking about just such an occurrence.

Sail up the Gulf of Bothnia, then go north through the scraggy spruce forests of Lapland to the Arctic Circle. There, under the Aurora Borealis and the midnight sun, lives a remarkable little dragon known to the Saami of Finland as the *turkis lisko*, or fur lizard. Cryptoherpetologists are only just beginning to understand this little fellow, but what they have learned has sent ripples through the draconic community.

Pels øgler and *päls ödlor*, in Norway and Sweden respectively, the *turkis liskoja* are native to the meagerly inhabited regions of northern Europe, from Finnmark to Lapland's interior, with rumors of sightings on Russia's Kola Peninsula, where they're known as the *zimnyaya drakony*,

or winter dragons. Snow-white in winter and licheny greenish-brown in the short summer months, they are perfectly adapted to the inhospitable wilds. Roughly 5 feet long—the size of a large wolverine (and often mistaken for one)—fur lizards have snow-shoe paws and a soft undercoat of hollow hairlike scales. Like musk ox fur, this acts as insulation against the elements, and tufting between their outer plates gives them a shaggy, bearish appearance. They also have wings and do not hesitate to tent them close when the winds howl and snows white out the stars.

Theirs is a nomadic environment, constantly following the seasons, and it affects not only their diet but also how they relate to the other creatures (including humans) around them. Distant, even aloof, they follow the tradition of early house dragons and serve more as exterior guardians than hearthside companions. Traveling with the peoples and herds of reindeer, they will keep other predators at bay, even take on bears if they must, to protect those in their charge. In exchange, if the occasional deer are culled from the herd, it is a small price to pay. They also enjoy the occasional taste of *Amanita muscaria,* more commonly known as fly amanita, a mushroom found in faërie rings in temperate and boreal regions. Though toxic even for Dragons, it is—as the shamans of the Saami will attest— a powerful hallucinogen. A mere nibble can provide trippy midwinter fun for all.

The unique thing about *turkis liskoja* (and what has given scientists pause) is that they live, work, and travel in families. All other house dragons are solitary creatures, paired at most. This is a practical adaptation: a passel of dragons can turn a cottage into cramped quarters in the blink of a gargoyle's eye. But these little ones flock together, sometimes in groups of as many as a score or more. Cryptoherpetologists believe this is an adaptation to both their environment and the needs of the people to whom they're attached. Living al fresco in frosty climes is a problem for any coldblooded creature. The long nights make it impossible for them to bask in the sun, so the few species who call the Arctic home have had to adapt. Hibernation is one way to go but is not an option if you're a house dragon with a duty to ward and warn. This is where numbers come in handy. A flight of *turkis* will huddle together, relying on each other to keep warm. When food is scarce, they will hunt together. And when the herds and humans in their charge are in danger, they will attack together.

Wolves, lynx, and even hungry bears don't stand a chance against such a draconic murmuration.

How long has this been going on? The people who know aren't saying, though some cryptoherpetologists guess back to Neolithic times. Surely the *liskoja's* detached nature, combined with vast lands and reticent humans, contributed to their staying off the draconic grid for so long. But times have changed. Miners and oilers have invaded their territory. The planet is warming, and the glaciers are in retreat. How all this will affect these delightful creatures, no one knows. Right now, we're just thrilled to be able to add the *turkis lisko* to our roster of dragons, to observe and learn from them, while we can.

Chapter Five
A BRIEF HISTORY OF DRAGONS

Istory is memory writ large, and Dragons have long memories.

Most people—even many an ardent dracophile—believe Dragon history began when our ancestors first saw them landing at the neighborhood water hole, scattering herds of elephants and quagga, crocodile floats, and leaps of leopards. And to an extent, they are right: history needs witnesses and a record of its passing. Its writing and telling imbues it with weight and truth. That said, if a Dragon soars through the forest and nobody sees it, is it really there? The answer is a resounding YES.

So, let's take a step back. Way back.

Long before *Homo sapiens* memorialized it on painted cave walls and petroglyphed cliffsides, the planet was full of life, including Dragons. In sea beds and tar pits, silt and amber, remnants of animals and plants long gone and utterly alien were everywhere. Insects with three-foot wingspans, sixteen-foot turtles, spade snouts, fishy tetrapods, and a treasure trove of dinosaurs—all left their mark. Since the sixth century BCE, scientists and mystics from Greece to China have deciphered fossil tales in both true and fanciful ways. Xenophanes of Colophon looked at a fossilized shell and saw a great sea flooding the earth, while over in Dragon-friendly China, dinosaur fossils—dragon bones—unearthed by pick and plow from the Sichuan Basin to Inner Mongolia were pulverized for medicines and carved into amulets. And in the 1800s, the sciences took a quantum leap forward to include the field of paleontology. Despite the vast millennia with which we're dealing, it's now possible for us to date even the most ancient fossil with remarkable accuracy. We now have a timeline for life on Earth dating all the way back to microbes in the primordial ooze, and subsequently,

a sense of our proper place in the grand, evolutionary scheme of things. Only the most rigid anti-science person will deny that pterosaurs caught thermals over the Tethys Sea a hundred million years ago or insist that stuffed archaeopteryx was a regular staple of Neanderthal cuisine. Great things, fossils ... except when it comes to Dragons.

Simply put, there are no Dragon fossils. Not a single one. The occasional sloughed scale, tooth, or claw has been found through the centuries, but not any legitimate fossils. Why? To the best of our understanding, we are dealing with a marvel of biochemistry. Basically, a Dragon produces sulfuric and perchloric acid as a byproduct of fire and flight. When killed in a sudden or violent way— acts of God or lost battles—these caustic fluids mix with richly elemental Dragon blood, resulting in volatile decomposition so rapid that fossilization is impossible. There is also the likelihood of considerable "spillage"— a lethal parting shot that has left many a Dragon slayer's victory Pyrrhic at best. But what of the Dragons who did not die in shock and gore? That remains a mystery, though the poetic consensus is that the Great Dragon welcomes them back to the stars.

Though no skeletal, winged quadruped will ever grace the great hall of the Smithsonian and thrill the hearts of millions, cryptopaleontologists are convinced that their ancestors—small, stubby, often wingless protodragons—date back to between 200 and 150 million years ago. They were smart and resilient; their mighty strands of draconic DNA survived feast, famine, and extinction-level events. They grew stronger, bigger—more Dragonish—with each passing eon.

They evolved.

Ancient Dragons

It's time to jump forward, to leave primordial chaos behind and enter an age when Dragons and human beings not only crossed paths but actually began to influence each other.

A hundred thousand years ago, Dragons squished their toes in the same Paleolithic mud our ancestors used to daub the wattle of their dwellings. They were essentially the Dragons we know today, if a bit larger; they had more room to grow. And as today, they were the apex predators, ruling land and sky with stream of flame and flash of fang.

Nietzsche said, "All great things must first wear terrifying and monstrous masks in order to inscribe themselves on the hearts of humanity" (Nietzsche, 2001). So it was with Dragons.

> All great things must first wear terrifying and monstrous masks in order to inscribe themselves on the hearts of humanity.
> —Friedrich Nietzsche, *Beyond Good and Evil*

To ancient humans, Dragons were harrowing mirrors of the untamed wilderness— of earthquakes, tempests, fire and flood, night and day, life and death. Their roar was thunder, their wings blotted out the sun. With teeth gnashing loud as a billion flints on stone, they would pluck mammoths from the steppes and aurochs from the veldt, scattering their bones like pick-up sticks to bleach in the sun.

Dragons were terror beasts who invaded dreams and shook the earth with awful majesty ... who clawed their way deep into our hearts.

But for those who looked on the world with less dread and more curiosity, with imagination and massive doses of wonder, Dragons were much, much more. They were masters of fire and the elements; bringers of rain, controllers of the tides, moon, even the stars. And, by

human standards, they were immortal. Mysterious and elemental, they not only inspired fear and trembling but also profound reverence. The Universe was theirs and they were Universal. Dragons were divine.

And why not? Back when scientific understanding was as rare as feathers on a wombat, the gods we created were our way to explain not only how we got here but what "here"—in all its inexplicable mystery—was. Paleolithic Earth was a scary, untamed place full of rapacious predators and mind-boggling natural phenomena. We needed chthonic deities more ineffable than the darkness they ruled, tutelaries more badass than the feral forces they battled. We needed Dragons.

Larger-than-life and wild as centuries are long, divinity poured off them like rain off their armored backs. They were naturals at being supernatural. And, without even asking if they wanted the gig, those who could get past the instinct to panic in their sublime presence turned Dragons into gods, Creators of the Cosmos who had been here since before time. They watched over land and sea, raising mountains, carving rivers, providing balance—black and white, good and evil—to a wild, eccentric planet. Chieftains sought their power; shamans sought their counsel. And when the people sat around the

fire, they would tell stories of the hunt, the gather, and the Dragons they saw on the way. In their magnificence, all truth was found, all prayers were answered. This was the beginning of Dragon lore, of our memories mingling with theirs.

Generation after generation, the stories were repeated, embellished, and refined until once-casual tales became holy writ, and a pantheon of sacred Dragons emerged. Lung, Aido Hwedo, Sovereign Plumed Serpent. They hatched from cosmic eggs and shaped the World and all her creatures with a word (or two).

These Dragons were, after all, literal movers and shakers, dynamic powers more than equal to the task. We honored them in their wildness with offerings and praise, and though size and nature made them hard to keep physically close, we kept them close in our hearts. In turn, they kept the natural world at bay, and if not at peace, at least in harmony, light with dark. Ophion, Ryu-jin, Alkha. Dragons were the gods who fit the times—gods who were not us.

This was a boon for the neighborhood enchantments, too. If the Dragons over the hill are dead ringers for the Creator of the Universe, you treat them with respect and

forgive the occasional missing cow or goat. At the very least, you give them a wide berth.

Unfortunately, even the most illustrious gods can wear out their welcome. As the centuries passed and we humans aspired to be civilized, chaos gave way to order, wattle to stone, and a sense of being attuned with the natural world to one of human entitlement and dominion. Some ten thousand years ago, we began to lose our use for scaly deities who could block out the sun and play catch with the moon. We needed more domestic gods for a more domestic world, gods with familiar faces who would not be out of place sharing hearth, board, or even bed.

New deities cropped up all around us: they had extended families—cosmically dysfunctional, as a rule—and were as fond of a feast as the next man. They advised heroes, scolded reprobates, and strengthened the blood of kings with their own. At best, these gods were our idealized selves, strong and wise, beautiful and loving, goodness personified and wrapped in celestial clouds we could only navigate in our dreams. At worst, they were carnival grotesques, petty and egocentric, scrappy and earth-shatteringly jealous. Some might even say diabolical. In short, human.

While we were making nice with these divine reflections or at least trying not to tick them off, what hap-

pened to the great Dragons who'd kept us safe for so long? It depended on where they lived.

In the East, Dragons essentially retained their positions of honor and reverence, especially among the rural peoples who counted on them for blessings and protection. They were also protected by the philosophical/spiritual nature of eastern faiths, far less dogmatic than those gestating in Mesopotamia, and soon to move west. Lao Tzu, Confucius, Buddha, not to mention numerous nameless shamans, may not all have embraced Dragons with the same degree of enthusiasm, but they were all open to the draconic experience. And so it was that while the Great Lung faded into the mists of legend, emperors continued to turn to Dragons for advice and even set up the first schools for Dragon Keeping. As for the more remote eastern enchantments, they lived on as Dragons should.

West of the Urals, things were very different. A few Dragons, like Ladon of ancient Greece, became cohorts and companions of the new gods. Ares had a particular fondness for Dragons, admiring their fierceness, embracing it as complement to his own martial inclinations; they, in return, guarded his shrines and sacred wells. More intriguing in its way is the theory among some scholars and Gnostics that Yahweh (as distinct from Elohim)

was/is himself a Dragon, an incarnation of the Canaanite Dragon god Yaw. This makes for an interesting twist on Moses's burning bush and thunderous admonitions from on high, on whirlwinds and even the destruction of Sodom and Gomorrah. Fire and brimstone sound a lot like Dragon fire to me.

Exceptions proving the rule, by and large we took their wondrous draconic feats (and our affections) and handed them to the new gods. Used hard and well, Cosmic Dragons of the west suddenly found themselves to be basilisks in a gecko world, too rough around the edges for civilized company. They were embarrassing reminders of our fearful, lizard-brain selves; their once majestic wildness deemed dangerous and even ugly next to deities who shared our personal aesthetic.

Replaced and unwanted, they were stripped of their divinity and burdened with our darkest fears and impulses; we stole their grace and blackened their souls. We turned them into monsters. If making gods is a noble exercise, making monsters is a much darker, more sinister endeavor. It is an act of ungrateful cruelty and willful neglect. Judgment, castigation, persecution, aloneness. These are the elements of monster-making, burnished through the centuries in rivers of blood.

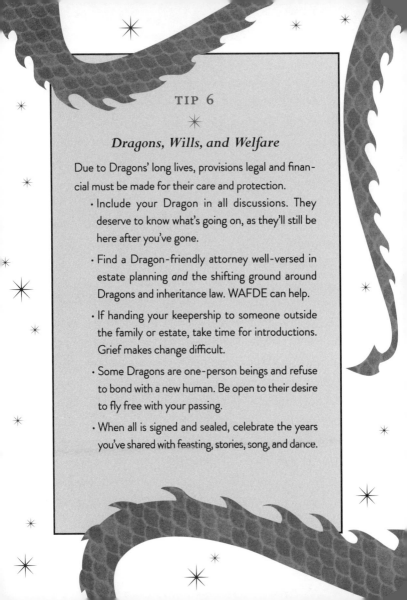

TIP 6

✳

Dragons, Wills, and Welfare

Due to Dragons' long lives, provisions legal and financial must be made for their care and protection.

- Include your Dragon in all discussions. They deserve to know what's going on, as they'll still be here after you've gone.

- Find a Dragon-friendly attorney well-versed in estate planning *and* the shifting ground around Dragons and inheritance law. WAFDE can help.

- If handing your keepership to someone outside the family or estate, take time for introductions. Grief makes change difficult.

- Some Dragons are one-person beings and refuse to bond with a new human. Be open to their desire to fly free with your passing.

- When all is signed and sealed, celebrate the years you've shared with feasting, stories, song, and dance.

Hero-kings were on the rise. Marduk, Enki, Cadmus, Thraetona. They needed quests and feats of glory to solidify their places as leaders of men. What better than to slay the old Dragon-gods, to clear the way for the new. One particular hero comes to mind: Keresaspa of ancient Mesopotamia. According to Sumerian lore, Keresaspa killed not one Dragon, but two. First, he took on Gandareva, a Dragon so large he stretched from the ocean depths to the stars above. Their battles lasted for days. Keresaspa was battered and blinded, his horses killed, his family abducted. But, in the end, human heroics triumphed and Gandareva was slain. Unfortunately, even the sweetest victories have consequences. Unbeknownst to Keresaspa, Gandareva watched over a far blacker, more dangerous Dragon, Azhi Dahaka. As the Zoroastrians tell it, after much rampaging and wanton feasting on cattle, camels, and humans, he was captured and imprisoned beneath Mount Demayand. There he stayed for centuries until, come the end times, he broke free. In a feat of Dragon-slayer/messianic bravado, Keresaspa returned to dispatch him and save the world.

Thus the new template for handling Dragons was set, and the course of Dragon history was changed. And for centuries, everything we thought we knew about them changed as well ... it had to.

Once upon a time, our ancestors knew Dragons were social beings with enchantments and weyrs that resembled human clans and villages. But it's hard to demonize someone you know has little ones waiting on supper back home. Where gods stand apart, monsters must be set apart. So, we abandoned Dragons out in the dark—not firing the way to the stars as they once did, but hungry and cold as the night itself. Facts be damned, we turned them into solitary creatures without kith, kin, or the joy of companionship, distanced from offering and hymn, from their place in the light. This was the story now told, the justification of the Dragon slayer: that they were ugly and cruel, rapacious and predatory. That they were Evil.

And as we know, it's a hero's duty—even his right—to destroy evil. Right?

Some Dragons chose to stand their ground and defend the weyrs they'd called home since before humans walked erect. Still more, especially those with young ones in tow, chose survival as the better part of valor. In what was to be the first recorded draconic diaspora, they left behind the world of men and withdrew deep into the wilderness. Of course, humans became the sole narrators of history

in their absence, and for millennia the lies about Dragons not only persisted—they grew.

Medieval Dragons: Christianity, the Dark Times, and the Great Migration

The history of Medieval Dragons is largely one of the Western weyrs. The isolating geography and politics of the East meant that, until the nineteenth century, Eastern Dragons might as well have been living on another planet, a place mysterious, secure, and protected. True, there were reports of draconic creatures ambling along the Silk Road or frolicking in the Yellow Sea off Hangzhou, Marco Polo's "City of Heaven," but such sightings were rare and the Dragons so fanciful by European standards as to be scarcely believed. And can you blame them? What's with all the whiskers? And where were their wings? To this day, scientists and philosophers alike lack a firm understanding of how great Eastern Dragons surf the clouds— imagine what a thirteenth-century Venetian must have thought!

We now look west, to Europe with its dark and gory ways. But it wasn't always like this. When Cadmus was sowing Dragon teeth in the hills of Boeotia, northern Europe was in a relatively Dragon-friendly phase. From Nordic fjords to the Iberian coast, Iron Age peoples had a live-and-let-live attitude toward the local enchantments. Dragons were their fierce but nonbelligerent neighbors—as long as they weren't provoked, that is. Druids and sages took the Dragon/human relationship even further. Much like their counterparts in the East, they respected Dragons as manifestations of Earth's elemental strength. Together they paced the ley-lines, connecting weyrs, sacred groves, wells, and standing stones with vibrant energy. They shared lore and tales of wood and spirit. Against skeptics and foes alike, the Druids welcomed Dragons fleeing persecution and defended them as learned mentors and kindred souls. Dragons and tribes had each other's backs when the need arose, which fortunately wasn't often ... until the age of Gaius Julius Caesar and the octopus that was ancient Rome.

Beginning around 50 BCE, Roman expansionism pushed north into Celtic lands and dealt tribes and weyrs many a heavy blow. Caesar and his ilk looked on Dragons with pragmatic, militaristic eyes, unencumbered by religious baggage. To the Roman mind, Dragons were not wicked per se but were definitely monstrous, uncontrollable beasts. And what Caesar couldn't control, he would destroy. The positive PR spin on his anti-Dragon campaign was the fact these creatures were standing in

the way of land and lucre. It didn't matter that neither land nor riches belonged to Rome in the first place, nor that by going after a weyr's precious metals and stones, they were actually threatening generations of hatchlings, the *true* Dragon treasure. But why let such petty considerations put a damper on empire building? Though the Celts and Druids did what they could to help, they were under siege themselves and had limited resources. In the end, the enchantments were on their own. By the time Hadrian erected his eponymous wall (122 CE), Dragons from the Apennine Mountains to Britannia's lake district, from the Tagus River to the Wadden Sea, had all but been driven to the fringes of human society. This suited Rome just fine. Their battles with the enchantments, especially those of Northern Gaul and Britannia, had been costly.

Dragons were Nature, and Nature was no longer Horace's "harmony in discord" with which they could coexist.

Bloody as these years were, they lacked the intense anti-Dragon zeal that was to wash over Europe like a tsunami as Christianity flowed out of the Middle East and conquered Rome.

Forget philosophical Greek Dragons, spiritual Dragons from India, Assyria, and Ur. Definitely forget the wise Dragons west of the Rhine and north of the Channel. Outside of a few small Gnostic circles, dualistic Christian thinking had no place for such forces, benevolent or otherwise. Dragons were Nature, and Nature was no longer Horace's "harmony in discord" with which they could coexist. It was chaos, wild, heathen, and misbegotten, there to be dominated and ruled, not accommodated and certainly not worshipped. Already on their way to full-on monster status, it took just a nudge to tip Dragons into Big Bad territory. With fangs bared, leathery wings unfurled, and licks of flame bronzing the clouds like sunset, it was not much of a leap to put them in Satan's shoes, to see them as daemonic stand-ins for the Prince of Darkness to be defeated in the name of the new faith. This was the heart and tainted soul of the Dragons-as-Devil movement—the driving force of the Dark Times. As John wrote in Revelation 20:1–2:

> And I saw an angel come down from heaven, having the key of the bottomless pit and a great chain

in his hand. And he laid hold on the dragon, that old serpent, which is the Devil, and Satan, and bound him a thousand years ... (King James Bible, 1974)

It's interesting to note that this tale was not exactly new; the names have been changed, but it is essentially the same as the apocalyptic account of Azhi Dahaka and Keresaspa.

Gentle as a lamb or sage as Solomon, it didn't matter. The Beast in Revelation was a hard image for any Dragon to counter.

Under the imperial patronage of Constantine the Great (272–337 CE), Christianity went from persecuted cult to dominant religion of Rome in a matter of decades. Unfortunately, this opened the way to proselytizing from one end of the Empire to the other. Celts and Picts, Goths and Vandals—even Vikings were converted. It had worked with the Romans, after all. And even among the most learned, very few evangelical monks were fluent in Dragon. Fewer still were willing to talk to what they considered Devil-monsters about saving their souls only to be laughed at or even singed for their efforts. And as the Church gained power, it became very brazen about

appropriating Pagan lands for their kirks, monasteries, and abbeys. These ley-rich lands not only encompassed sacred groves and wells, but neighboring weyrs as well. Of course, expecting enchantments to surrender their ancestral homes to a faith that loathed them was a real non-starter. Even the most open-minded monks knew that no matter how politely they asked, Dragons were not going to simply pack up and move. Better to just do away with them entirely.

While standing before gods makes us small, taking on monsters makes us noble and heroic. And killing a Dragon for God makes you positively saintly. Thus, following the example of George in fourth-century Cappadocia and gathering steam with Patrick chasing the snakes—i.e., Druids and Dragons—from Hibernia, by the fifth century the second wave of draconic persecution descended upon the European enchantments with a vengeance. The list of Dragon slayers is daunting: Michael, Margaret, Clement, Samson, Romain of Rouen, Philip the Apostle, Keyne of Cornwall, and those known in Dragon studies circles as the French Quintet: Martha, Florent, Cado, Maudet, and Pol. The results of their deeds were devastating to Dragons both True and pseudo-. In fact, if the stories and art of the time are any indication, most of the Dragon

kills claimed by saints were aspises or young wyverns caught in dracophobic crossfire.

As the first millennium neared its end, anti-Dragon sentiments in Europe became epidemic. Religious dogma had supplanted the magic of Druidic lore. Augmented by the approaching thousand-year deadline of John's Revelation, superstition spread among clerics and farmers, knights and merchants. It was a black and white world; with the Apocalypse just around the corner, Dragons were as black as a starless night. The Dark Ages were bleak, and humans needed someone—something—to blame for plagues and blighted crops, lost calves and deadly frosts. In this harsh time, the Dragons' jaw-dropping awesomeness became a thing of the past. They were instead manifestations of our inner daemons, receptacles of our fears. Not eager to confront the former, the latter won out.

We do terrible things when we are afraid. And then we make up stories to rationalize our horrors. With Dragons the tales followed a familiar plot. They were servants of the Devil and, like their master, treacherous monsters, wantonly threatening herd and home. They demanded tribute—fair maidens, preferably of royal blood—and would devour them with relish. But since a feast was as good as a farthing, they would also dine on anyone else

who crossed their paths. All this was utter rubbish, of course. Anyone who bothers to ask knows that Dragons don't much like the taste of humans. They think we're far too stringy and not a bit like chicken.

Still, justifications must be made, fears exploited, and anti-Dragon sentiments stoked. Only then could their persecution continue.

In the Dragon wars of the ninth and tenth centuries, the young and the very old were particularly vulnerable. With deaths too numerous to count, enchantments were worn down and burnt out. Loss has a way of doing that.

Though some were tempted to go all out anti-human, wiser heads prevailed. Survival was more important than revenge. Offered refuge among the fae, many retreated into the mists of the Otherworld to wait out the madness. Many more decided they'd had enough: they were done with Europe. Taking wing, they flew north and west, bouncing off Iceland and making their way to the New World. There they cavorted and mingled with the indigenous Dragons and started anew. This is known as the Trans-Atlantic Transmigration.

Despite all the prophecies of doom and gloom, the calendar hit 1001 and the world did not end. Unfortunately, the new millennium opened on a Europe that was essentially Dragon-free for all save the most ardent dracophiles. Only believers in the rare and mysterious could hope to spot them through the mists. For the rest, Dragons became fictions, villains in heroic epics and monsters in faërie tales. Pseudodragons filled the ensuing void as best they could, becoming the subjects of alchemical experiments (though they proved poor substitutes for the Real Thing) and pawns in local disputes such as the gargoyle wars of Champagne and the Loire Valley. This was the status quo for centuries to come, the legacy of the Dark Times.

But was this period of violence and misunderstanding the only story? Hardly. There were those who held to a different memory of Dragons who refused to forget their power and wisdom. They kept the valor and strength of Dragons alive in heraldic devices, especially in Celtic lands. Cities from London to Poole have rampant Dragons silver, gold, and even blue on their coats of arms; the Kings of Aragon and Braganza sported wyverns on their helmets. And of course, there was Y Ddraig Goch, the Red Dragon of Wales. A creature out of legend, he knew

Merlin in his time and raced across King Arthur's royal standard. His likeness was carried into battle for centuries, a symbol of sovereign authority from Richard I in the Third Crusade to Henry V at the Battle of Agincourt, where Welsh longbowmen saved the day. When Richard III fell on Bosworth Field in 1485, the Welsh Henry VII became the first Tudor king of England. To honor his heritage and the power of the Dragon, he placed Y Ddraig Goch opposite the English lion on the royal coat of arms. There he remained until 1603, when James Stuart—never a fan of the Tudors—ascended the throne and replaced the Dragon with the Scottish unicorn.

As for the Welsh, they never gave up on Y Ddraig Goch; he is emblazoned on their flag to this day. This, too, is a legacy of the Dark Times.

Enlightenment and Return: Dragons in our Modern Age

We now arrive at today … or almost today. The darkness of the Middle Ages did lighten in the Renaissance. For art and science, it was indeed a rebirth, but not for Dragons. Religion was still the compass guiding most people's lives and Christianity's official position on our scaly friends remained unchanged, at least symbolically speaking. Priest to Pope, the Church fathers had long since ceased

seeing real Dragons. They were more concerned with princes, politics, and consolidating power. Only the occasional mystic like Francis of Assisi, Julian of Norwich, and Meister Eckhart, had the temperament to break through the mists protecting the refugee enchantments. Unfortunately, there is scant record of what they might have found there, though whether it is due to personal choice or censorship from an outside source is anyone's guess. I lean toward the latter: with their visions and personal connections to the divine, mystics had a way of putting authority's snout out of joint. Francis holds a place of honor among weyrs around the world, and his feast day (October 4) is considered a holiday among Dragons throughout Europe. It is also interesting to note that the city of Norwich is currently home to an annual Dragon festival. I like to think Julian would approve.

Despite the glories of the Renaissance, scarcely a year went by without a battle, revolt, or all-out war somewhere on the continent. Indeed, it can be said that the Renaissance is bracketed by the Hundred Years' War at the start (1337–1454) and the Thirty Years' War at the end (1618–1648). In between there was the rise of Protestantism, followed by over a hundred years of religious purges and persecutions. With such madness swirling all about, was it any wonder Dragons stayed out of the fray?

Western Dragons weren't the only ones at odds with Europeans. Spanish and Portuguese colonization of the New World brought the Inca, Aztec, and numerous less well-known peoples to ruin. The conquistadors' quest for gold also put them on a collision course with the indigenous Dragons. The shy Feathered Dragons south of the thirty-fourth parallel were hit hardest, and, under extreme distress, they vanished into the rainforested beyond where they remain to this day. It didn't matter on which side of the Atlantic they lived, nor if they were feathered or scaled. Dragons were still expendable.

Despite occasional sightings here and there, now and then, European Dragons didn't catch a real break until the post-Enlightenment dawn of what we might call "modern times."

Sapere aude!—dare to know. Dare to be wise. Dare to think for yourself. This was Immanuel Kant's challenge to eighteenth-century Europe, one Dragons surely

*Sapere aude!—
dare to know.
Dare to be wise.
Dare to think
for yourself.*

echoed from the shadows. It was answered by people setting reason before superstition and science before unquestioning faith. Church was separated from state, and progress and tolerance became guiding principles of the creative and intellectually curious. Nothing could have pleased Dragons more.

By the mid-nineteenth century, scaly snouts were poking through the mists. Mouths open, they flehmed, tasting the temper of the societies around them. Things had changed a lot since they were last out and about. Villages were now cities crowded with people and industry; groves were gone, waters were poisoned, and the air was thick with soot and dingy smoke. But the biggest surprise was the people.

Gone were the Dragon slayers of yore. In their place were Newton and Darwin, revolutionizing the way people looked at the sciences, including the age of the Earth and the beings on it. Fossil hunters and their finds opened minds to the possibility of all sorts of previously unimagined creatures. Best of all were the mystics, spiritualists, and artists who longed to bring back the magic and wonder of ancient times. This led to a Druidic renaissance. And no one loved or understood Western Dragons like the Druids.

For the Dragons, this was just the entrée they had waited centuries for. Setting ancient wounds and past grudges aside, they took it.

Personally, from all my talk with enchantments over the years, I've come to believe Dragons returned to the world because, looking around, they knew we needed them … badly. We needed their special brand of wonder and magic, and over the past 150 years, that need has only grown. Even at the nightmarish height of the Dark Times, I doubt Dragons could have imagined what we've become or how horrifically we've treated each other and the planet: world wars, genocides, atomic weapons, continents of refuse polluting the oceans, and climate change the likes of which hasn't been seen since the Cenozoic Era.

This may well be their last-ditch effort to set us straight. To burnish our memories until they shine like golden scales in the sun. to remind us that buried deep in discord, harmony still exists.

Chapter Six

ONCE UPON
A DRAGON

Long before cell phones and computers; before movies, radio, television; before even books, when language itself was in its infancy, our ancestors came together for fun and fellowship at day's end. In the gathering dusk, they sat around the fire that kept darkness and danger at bay. In the silence, sages gazed through the flames into the night. Staring back from the wilderness were eyes bright as the stars and deep as the space between them: Dragons ... with stories to tell.

This was the beginning of once-upon-a-time, the realm where all things are possible. Where Dragons live forever and die in an instant; where they are named and nameless, villains and heroes. Where Dragons become symbols even larger than their already out-sized selves. Symbols of the Universe, at its best and worst. Of us, at our best and worst. Once-upon-a-time. Where Dragons rule.

No book about Dragons would be complete without a visit to this land, with tales from East and West. (Unfortunately, the Feathered Dragons insist on keeping their stories to themselves.) Following are tales about Dragons, sometimes even told by Dragons. These are fabulous beings (of course all Dragons are *fab-u-lous!*) and they'd relish their narratives, true as they might be, being taken as legend or even myth rather than historical fact.

So grab a spot by the fire, lose yourself in the Dragons dancing among the embers, and enjoy.

The Dragon Who Ate the Sun

Many centuries ago, according to those who were there, a great Blue Dragon lived in the north of Asia, thousands of *li* beyond the Heilong—Black Dragon—River. His home was in the bowels of Shèngli, a mountain covered with ice and planted with frozen fire. It hadn't always been so bleak. Once, herds of fat caribou and families of mam-

moths wandered the hills. Rabbits romped through grassy valleys, and swallows murmured and dove among willow and birch. But that was long ago, when Blue Dragon was young ... before he caught a chill and everything changed.

Seemed such a silly thing, a Dragon with a cold. But even lying in the mouth of his lair and basking in the late-summer rays, he could not shake the aches and chill in his bones.

He gazed into the sky and sighed. The sun was so warm, so inviting, but so far away. If only he could touch that glorious heat ... just gobble it all up. The longer he thought about it, the more irresistible the idea became. With a sneeze and a sniffle, he rattled his scales and rose up into the heavens. He hitched a ride on the solar winds, past moon and morning star, until he could feel the blush of the corona against his whiskers. With the flick of his tongue, he inhaled a white-hot mouthful of plasma.

Swee-eet! Blue Dragon had never tasted anything like it, all silk worms and green papaya, osmanthus, lime leaves, and pearls wrapped in sea petals. It burned out his shivers, too. He smiled. A Dragon could get used to this.

And he did. For the next thousand years—Dragons were even longer-lived back then—he was a slave to his appetites. He hungered. He flew back and forth, streaking

through space like a comet, to dine on the raw energy of the sun, returning home for a brief rest before taking off again. He ate and ate and grew and grew until he became the largest Dragon in the world. The fire in his belly not only kept him warm but burnished his scales, turning them from cool blue to incandescent gold. Skimming past the moon, he caught his reflection in the Serpent Sea and smiled. Gold Dragon—he liked it.

The Dragon was so busy admiring his new physique and stuffing his maw with hydrogen flares that he was oblivious to the consequences of his gluttony. Warm and full and brilliant gold, he did not notice that the Earth was spinning beneath a sun shriveling, browning like a moldering peach.

The days turned bitterly dark; a creeping freeze poured down from the poles; glaciers rolled over the steppes, killing off beasts and birds and driving those who survived towards the equator. And the Yellow Emperor was furious. It was mid-summer, yet he was wearing so many layers of fur and silk he could barely move. Desperate for answers—and an orange not frozen to a tree—he summoned Yan Wei-Long, Master Astronomer and Dragon Lord, to his chamber.

"Well?" he demanded through chattering teeth.

TIP 7

Dragon Safety and Etiquette

- Never turn your back on a strange Dragon.

- Boundaries have their place, and *no* isn't a dirty word when training. Limits keep everyone safe and go far in keeping home-repair costs in check.

- Always celebrate your Dragon's Hatching Day and Remembrance-of-Name Day.

- When riding your Dragon remember three simple rules: No bridle or saddle; dress warm; and pack your passport and flying license.

- Dragons and their people are ambassadors to a fragile, frequently hostile world. Heed local laws at all times and, if asked to leave, don't make a fuss.

"Shèngshàng." Wei-Long bowed low. "I have studied the skies, Exalted One. Comet comings and goings, shooting stars and the fading sun. And I talked at length with Kiau-Long, Dragon of the Southern Sea."

"And? What did she say?" The Emperor paced back and forth, tapping his staff impatiently. Dragon keepers never got to the point.

The Dragon Lord paused. Wise as the Emperor was, he did not always understand Dragons. And Kiau-Long's words were a mix of incredible rumor and hearsay gathered from across the seas. They were hard for even him, a keeper who knew so many of her kind, to believe. If he told the Emperor that the Great Blue had been devouring the sun or that he'd turned quite gold with feasting and was now grounded somewhere up north, the Exalted One would think he'd lost his Dragon-loving mind.

Wei-Long cleared his throat. "The Great Blue Dragon is not well," he said, as if that explained everything. "He caught a cold."

The Emperor stared. "And your Emperor is catching pneumonia." Blue Dragon! He should have known a Dragon was involved. "You are my Dragon Lord, Wei-Long. Fix it. Fix it before the whole world freezes solid."

chapter six

138

Always prepared, Wei-Long had packed his cases before going off to the palace: vats of potions and salves, sacks of herbs and pots of gingered honey ... everything a Dragon keeper might need, including a cage full of a thousand swallows covered against the cold. Now at the Emperor's order, he loaded everything and himself on the back of a bronze Dragon he'd recently cured of a nasty case of gout, and headed due north, as the Dragon flies.

Through dark days and wintry wastes, they travelled, watching the sky for the faintest sign of a sun-eating Dragon. The Heilong River was iced so thick, they could cross it without so much as a crack beneath weighty bronze claws. At the crook of the River Lena where it licked the polar ridge, they turned east, up the valley towards Shèngli. It was the tallest mountain between the desert and the Northern Sea, and, despite all the eternal cold and darkness, its slopes were awash with a warm aureate glow.

As they got closer, the ground rumbled and a plaintive wail thickened the air.

The Gold Dragon lay prostrate in front of his lair, moaning and groaning like the most miserable creature in the world. His massive distended belly rippled high as the foothills and thundered like a volcano about to blow.

"Grrrowwruuu-rhooo-ohhh," he moaned, holding his stomach tight and rocking back and forth.

Wei-Long whistled long and low between his teeth. He didn't have to be a Dragon keeper to know the poor creature had a very sick tummy. "Oh, Gold Dragon," he sighed. "What have you done to yourself?"

"Rhuuuuu-ohhh."

"I can imagine. Ate too much, did we?"

He nodded.

"Got a case of solar heartburn?"

Bronze Dragon was about to laugh, but Wei-Long shot her a look. It isn't nice to laugh at a Dragon in distress, even if he brought it on himself.

"And you've made a mess for the rest of us, too. What if we help each other?"

"Oh please, yes. Anything you want. Just ask."

"Don't worry, I will."

Now, while any reasonably astute human can spot a Dragon with a belly ache, it takes a proper Dragon keeper to know how to treat him. Yan Wei-Long was just such a person, as was his father before him. He knew Dragon likes and dislikes, wants and needs, good traits and bad habits, and how to sort them when something

went wrong ... even as spectacularly wrong as it had with Gold Dragon.

He took a vat of snapdragon and ginger tea and set it near the Dragon to warm. "You have been a very naughty Dragon, eating the sun like that. You thought it noble nourishment, no doubt, but you went too far." He unpacked the swallows, too. "You forgot the rest of the Universe, and it turned on you."

Chastened, the Dragon groaned.

"The only way all of us get better is if you put the sun back in the sky, where it belongs."

"But—but—I'll starve."

"Nonsense, Dragon. Have you forgotten all the wonderful things Dragons like to eat? Bamboo, lotus blossoms."

"Yuck, vegetables."

As every keeper knows, when common sense fails, try bribery. "Perhaps you'd prefer a rare, old delicacy ..." Wei-Long uncovered the cage full of birds. "One thousand swallows. Food of gods and Dragons. I will trade you one swallow for a year's worth of sunshine."

Gold Dragon started counting the birds, but they hopped and flitted so much he soon lost track.

"A thousand, you promise?"

"You have the word of Yan Wei-Long, Dragon Lord."

chapter six

"Ahh—I've heard of you, Dragon Lord. Ooogrrr-shuuu!" He grabbed his belly and yowled. "All right, all right. You win. But I don't know how to give it back. You have to help me."

"That's why I'm here." Wei-Long dipped a finger in the tea to make sure it was warm enough. "Drink this, Dragon."

"No no no. That's madness. It will put out my fire."

"Trust me, Dragon. Just drink it. All of it."

He took a sip. "Could use some honey."

Yan ladled three scoops of ginger honey into the tea. Gold Dragon raised a pleading brow; Yan added one more.

The Dragon drained the tea, every drop. "Well?"

"A little patience." And the Dragon keeper stepped back, way back.

"Will I stay golde—" A rumble deep in his stomach interrupted his thought as waves rippled through his underscales.

"Ooo . . . ooo . . . what did you *do* to me?!"

Head back, he opened his mouth and let loose the longest, loudest belch the Universe had ever heard. A stream of burning hydrogen erupted into the heavens. Thirty-five *kè* later (eight and a half minutes, more or less) the sun

flamed to life. Mid-summer heat, dry as cricket wings, radiated back to Earth with a warming vengeance.

"Great Long's whiskers!" gasped the Dragon. "That was—wow!" He shook himself, tip to tail, then pretzeled himself around, took a long look, and smiled. He was still golden. And he was hungry.

As icicles began drip-dripping from the mouth of his lair, the Gold Dragon picnicked on swallows roasted to an amber turn. He could have stuffed himself silly, eating every one of the promised thousand, but, half-way in, a glance at Wei-Long gave him pause. He had been foolish and greedy before and wasn't going to make that mistake again. He pushed the platter of swallows towards his guests, taking a pawful of lemongrass instead.

"Great Long's whiskers!" gasped the Dragon. "That was—wow!"

When, in the torrid *sanfu* days of late summer, Wei-Long returned home to Panyu, the Emperor presented him with the Order to the Blue Dragon in honor of his keeper's wisdom and ingenuity. And, from that day forward, a great Golden Dragon adorned all the imperial robes, a humbling reminder for the Emperor to keep his appetites in check and to always put the needs of his people before his own desires.

When the Wyrm Turns: One Dragon's Beowulf

I was hatched. All Dragons are. Long after the enchantments were driven out of the Levantine deserts into Europe, I popped out of my egg, itching to be all noble and heroic. Humans don't often think of Dragons as heroes, but we are in our way. In our stories.

My family lived in Druid lands within a whiff of the sea, though I don't remember exactly where. (I was only a velvet-winged dragonlet back then; the specifics have grown hazy with time.) When Romans ravaged the sacred woods of Gaul with their tromping boots and iron spears, the enchantments took to the winds to fight or flee. My family fought. My mother, father, three brothers, and a flurry of kin were killed protecting the standing stones of Carnac from the barbarian legions. I escaped, flying north until the loss became small dots of memory I could almost ignore. Yet I have nightmares still.

Lake Vänern was vast and abounding with enough fish for a weyr full of Dragons. The woods round about were

thick with elk and hare, beaver and grouse. I found a cavern deep and dry with chambers veined with gold. As my mother said, "Find yourself a pile of gold and sit on it." So I did. (I passed her advice on to Grendel, but things didn't work out so well for him.) A puff of Dragon breath made it perfectly cozy.

Best of all, the nearest humans were far, far away. They preferred to keep to their ships and the sea coast rather than sweet-water shores, which suited me down to the least of my mossy-green scales. The seasons passed and I was content. Not that I was entirely alone: now and then I'd cross paths with transient Dragons from the east. Brief greetings, a whisker-wag over roasted salmon, then they were gone. That suited me too. Get close to Dragons and you can't help but care for them. And care means loss. I'd known enough loss for a hundred Dragon lifetimes. I chose this solitary life. I found peace.

Unfortunately, peace never lasts. In time, the sea people came inland, scruffy and bearded, with ax and pick and greed for gold. They built a long house, all logs and sod—barely enough to keep the snows out—and one house became two, two became four, until they had a weyr of their very own. They fished my lake, hunted my forest, and mined my hills. But as long as they stayed clear of my

cave, I paid them little mind. They were few in number and more nuisance than danger, not like the Romans.

They also had a healthy respect for Dragons, unlike the Romans. They would gift me with the occasional goat or one of their six-horned rams. Rich and fatty, such treats were a nice change from my usual fare. And their metalsmiths would leave bowls of beaten gold and silver; a little lumpy for sleeping, but I appreciated the gesture. We found a way to coexist and, for years, it was good.

Grendel's murder was a shock, bloody, beastly, and cruel. We did not know each other well, but I liked him. He had a fierce, almost Dragonish quality to him, raw and rough about the edges, different from most two-legs. In my experience, humans don't often like different. So much easier to fear and shun, exile to the wastelands. Call in a hero when things go wrong. Small hearts. Limited imaginations. Bah! Hrothgar never tried to understand Grendel or envision what such aloneness would do to him. Beowulf, well … he was just a glory-hound, wasn't he? And they call Dragons monsters.

I see the wheels turning. You're putting the pieces together—Beowulf and Grendel. A Dragon. You're Dragon people, you've heard this story before: Beowulf's tale, all sprung verse and Nordic swagger. Or so you think.

I am the Dragon and this is my tale. The right tale.

Grendel's death—how long ago was that? The years bleed one into another; I have lost count. Ten, twenty, fifty. The exact number escapes me. The memory of that marvelous wild creature was all but fading from my mind when a series of events brought it back, crystal as the river-run in spring.

It all began when a ragged band of men ambled north from the coast. They were coarser than the others, with battle-scored faces and sword-calloused hands. Mercenaries. Soldiers, if you prefer, once upon a time. Never trust soldiers. Still, there was no enemy here. And soldiers get bored with no one to kill; in time they'd move along. So, I retired to my cave to sleep and wait. I was a Dragon; I could outwait them all.

And I would have, gladly, had one of the shabbies not disturbed my slumber. No doubt he heard rumors or a mead-soaked tale of the Lake Vänern Dragon and his glittering hoard. More myth than truth, but lure enough for a human looking for riches. ("His!" Hmph! Silly humans always assume a lone Dragon is male. I'm not, of course, but they never asked.)

Worse than a troll at mid-summer, the rogue stank of stale fish and peat fire. Might as well have been clanging

chapter six

147

bells and blowing whistles as he rifled through my home. He picked up a golden bowl and without so much as a Dragon-may-I, tucked it into his bag. One bauble, more or less, why did I bother? I could say because if I let him get away, others would follow. And it would be true. But more true is that beneath these verdant scales, I am a sentimental Dragon, and the fool stole the first gift the village smiths ever gave me.

So I stopped him, as was my right. Tough, stringy little thief.

Humans make such a fuss about Dragon justice. You'd think I'd blackened the fields and burnt the whole kingdom to cinders ... not that I would, of course. Just defending my home, my possessions. All very proportionate. How was I to know he had such famous friends?

Beowulf was an old man when I met him. I'd heard of him, of course, of his hand in slaying Grendel and his vengeful mum. He was much younger, then. Fitter. He might have been a challenge. Then. Now his beard was grey, his arms heavy and bowed under sword and shield. His shoulders, though still broad, bore a disheartened hunch. Not much of the bear he once was. Time wears even legends down. I should know.

Yet, with naked steel, he barged into my cave, crying for my hot Dragon head. He stood before me, the grizzled king of the Geats, looking for a final "heroic" deed, a last notch on the hilt of his gem-crusted sword. Looking for one last dance with Death. Fool.

At least that's what he said. He was a talker, Beowulf. Wanted everything out there in epic form. I half-expected to find a frightened scribe hiding in the shadows, taking down every word for posterity.

He boasted of past gories, of battles won and trophies taken. Grendel stood atop his list. The kill that made him king. His finest hour.

Men and their monsters.

I could have killed him for that alone. After all, Grendel was as much my friend as the thief was his. If I bore skin instead of scales, they'd call me just, even heroic. I told him this, but he only stared. Basic Dragonish was obviously not included in kingship lessons. Fortunately, we Dragons know many tongues.

"I have no need of your crowing, Bear," I roared in my best Geatish. "Go away. You do not belong here."

"Dragon, you broke the peace."

chapter six

149

"You lie, king! It was my peace that was broken. My home invaded. Is not a Dragon's lair her castle?"

"That may be," he replied, "but you ate one of my men."

"Your man was a thief."

"We all have our faults. I am his king; he's under my protection. I may not have much time, but I would see my land in peace before I give up my crown. I would see civilization survive. I don't expect you to understand. What can a Dragon possibly understand about the duties of kingship, the need of legacy?"

I growled at his arrogance. Dragons were risking their lives for weyr and kin long before humans swung down from the trees. "Great Geat!" I laughed. "Civilization is overrated. Get out while you can."

"I am Beowulf."

"And I am a Dragon. But I do not wish to kill you today. I hear your muscles strain, your bones creak with age. Perhaps when you were younger, we might have had a contest, then. A right epic battle. The stars would have sung of it long after the sun burned black and the earth grew cold. Not now. Now I am Death, and you cannot beat me. So go!"

His eyes blazed. "I cannot," he rasped defiantly.

He had courage, the mad courage of those so close to death they no longer fear it. The freedom that comes with nothing to lose. He wouldn't leave and couldn't win. In that moment, he was probably the most dangerous human I'd ever known.

What followed was a blur of steel and fire and flash of fang. Who would have thought the old man could move so fast? Or that his blade could be so sharp? Still, I was a Dragon. Scale nicks and chips were nothing compared to the life flowing from his chest and brow. Such a delicate mortal.

Bleeding and scorched, he slumped against the wall. "I ... yield, Dragon!" he huffed. "Mercy."

"Mercy is for the civilized," I growled. "And Dragons are not that, you say. Mercy! Did your kind show mercy to my family in Gaul? Or you, king, to Grendel? I told you to leave. That was my mercy. Now that you've lost your last battle, would you have more?"

A ragged breath was his only reply.

"You're dying, king."

A wan light flickered in his eyes; he tried to smile. "I had no choice. You do understand."

Towering over him, strong and triumphant though I was, I felt a sadness knot my throat. I too had lost.

chapter six

151

"I understand far more than you humans will ever know," I said. "I understand that there is grace in wildness and victory in retreat. That Dragon souls are ancient and our hearts breakable as ice in spring. I understand that I can't stay here. No tribe lets their king's death go unavenged. Armies would be raised, blades edged. Soldiers by the hundreds would clamber for my head. There would be no peace for any of us.

"I will not live that way. I grant you your wish, Beowulf: Dragon mercy. When your people come for you, I'll be gone. They will believe you slew me, the evil Dragon of Death. It is expected, after all, you being their hero. With your last breath, you preserved the peace, as a king should. Your legacy is secure. Your people will thrive, and your story with them. Embellished, no doubt, with time. Perhaps you can beat Death after all."

Without so much as a glance over my tail, I left hearth and hoard and followed the moon into the west. Three days later I came to rest among dappled Snow Dragons playing

It's good to remember—
to tell our truths.
To be the hero in
a ragged world.

along the shores of a brave new world. I was a weary immigrant in search of refuge, and their welcome was warm, their questions few. They became my new family.

I hadn't thought of my old life in goblin's years, not until Dragon ships rose with the sun over the horizon and it all came back.

It's good to remember—to tell our truths. To be the hero in a ragged world.

Chapter Seven
LIVING WITH DRAGONS

It should come as no surprise to dracophiles that all Dragons, True and pseudo-, are endangered. Like many species—except on a larger scale—Dragons are at odds with virtually everything in the modern world ... not least of which are us. Our numbers, greed, politics, and rampant carelessness with this fragile planet are wiping out species left and right, threatening many others. Those most in conflict with mankind, and thus the most vulnerable, are the last of the megafauna (elephants, rhinos,

whales) and top predators (big cats, bears, wolves). Dragons are not only the mega-est of the megafauna but are also apex predators bar none.

We may push tigers and yetis to the brink of extinction, but Dragons will not be pushed—not again. They have as much right to this Earth as we do and will remind us of it with fang and flame if need be. Resolute they stand, claws planted deep in terra firma, ready to take on all poachers and miners, polluters and builders, any who would do them harm. Yet, they are sapient beings, wiser than most people I know. And in their wisdom, they know all-out war with humans and our modern weaponry is sheer madness. Better to enlist allies among us two-legs and find safe haven in sanctuary, lay-by, and among Dragon keepers.

Sanctuaries and Lay-Bys

Ursula K. Le Guin, a woman well acquainted with Dragons, wisely wrote that "it is one thing to read about dragons and another to meet them" (Le Guin, 1972). Today, sanctuaries and lay-bys are among the most natural and eco-friendly ways to experience the truth of her words.

Dragon sanctuaries are an ancient idea, refined through the years. The first was established by a guilty Apollo in the Pindus Mountains as a place to ward and raise the last clutch laid by Python, prophetic Dragon of Delphi, whom he slew. He gave her eggs into the care of Epirotes, a most generous Dragon who saw the brood grow and multiply into one of the greatest weyrs in the Mediterranean. It's conservation at its best, or so they say.

Modern Dragon sanctuaries began cropping up in the early twentieth century under the umbrella of the Dragon Conservancy Program. They're not as flashy as the golden garden of Epirotes, but they are bold conservation efforts, nonetheless. Like the Yukon Delta Wildlife Refuge or the much smaller Tarcu Mountains Reserve in Romania, or the myriad parks and reserves around the globe, they offer Dragons safe and inviting habitats. They also provide hunting grounds diverse and plentiful, which prevents clashing with farmers over lost cows or sheep. Sanctuary enchantments have a buffer between themselves and humanity; they roam free, as the Great Dragon intended.

Scientists and civilians alike are welcome to observe under the strictest of supervision. Which is as it should be. These are wild Dragons and the sanctuaries are their homes. We certainly wouldn't like strange creatures crashing through our living rooms without care or regard. Why should they? But, if you are up for keeping your distance and following the rules, a visit to Dragon country will not only enlighten, but also provide a much-welcome infusion of awe and understanding between species. Plus, all fees go toward education and anti-poaching programs. Not that Dragons need a lot of help with poachers; fire and fang usually do the job. But, when we need to step in, the funds are there, and enchantments sleep easier.

Sanctuary ABCs

1. You are in Dragon Country. It's their home. Act accordingly.

2. Stay with your guide and group. Wandering off can be hazardous, especially during mating and hatching seasons.

3. Leave your litigious instincts at the gate. The law of the Sanctuary always favors the Dragons. If something nasty happens, suck it up. You're on your own.

4. Open your eyes and go forth. You'll have an unforgettable adventure.

For the past fifty years, the World Association for Dragons Everywhere (WAFDE), in conjunction with the International Dragon Conservancy (IDC) and local Dragon orga-

nizations, has been working tirelessly to designate every known weyr a sanctuary space. These preservation efforts are not only good for Dragons, but good for the planet, as well. WAFDE has also been engaged in outreach work through their ADD (Adopt-A-Dragon) and KFD (Kids for Dragons) Programs. ADD models itself after similar undertakings by the WWF (World Wildlife Fund), where for a nominal sum, you can "adopt" a Dragon, complete with a certificate of weyr appreciation. All fees go right back to the sanctuaries and other conservation efforts. Young minds being most receptive to the strange and unusual, KFD targets the next generation through schools and youth organizations with children aged eleven and older, facilitating group "adoptions" and even field trips to local sanctuaries or Dragon estates. Both of these efforts have been met with grow-ing enthusiasm, indicating that draconic appreciation is winning against ancestral draconic fear. Cause for cel-ebration all around.

But it is one thing to read about dragons and another to meet them.
—Ursula K. Le Guin,
A Wizard of Earthsea

If you're up for a more intimate draconic experience than a supervised trek through the wilderness, but not inclined to full-on Dragon keeping, a Dragon lay-by might be just the thing.

Lay-bys are a network of Dragon-friendly wilderness areas where itinerant Dragons can go and snatch a meal, a drink, and a rest before moving on. They can also be miniature edens for indigenous flora and fauna. The basics are far from complicated: forty-plus acres of game-rich woodland (the more the merrier); a sweet-water source, preferably a lake or river with a thriving fish population and deep enough for bathing; simple shelter from the elements; and finally, patience.

Before you jump into lay-by building, do your research. Know your piece of the world, including weather extremes and the needs of both your neighborhood Dragons and those who might pass through for fun or seasonal relocation. The latter has become particularly important in areas hit hard by the escalating effects of climate change: desert Dragons struggling under prolonged droughts, coastal Dragons seeing their weyrs threatened by rising tides and severe storms, and polar Dragons losing food and homes to calved glaciers and melting icecaps. Such changes to habitat inspire Dragons—especially juveniles with lots of energy—to explore foreign lands with a mind to future relocation, if they must. When in doubt about anything, contact your local WAFDE chapter. They will be able to help.

Dragons are omnivores, so plan accordingly. Vegetation is as important as prey, so plant with a mind to both edible greens and berries, nuts, fungi, and fruits. That said, ordinary vegetable gardens and orchards, while appreciated, are more domestic than necessary. Better to intersperse an apple tree here and there among the hawthorns, or a patch of wild sage among the heather. If your family harvest is abundant and you want to share, the occasional cache of veggies near the lay-by's shelter will always be appreciated. The same rule applies to giving them access to livestock vs. standard fish or game. Though helpful in particularly lean times, you don't want to make your visitors reliant on human handouts. Remember, you're dealing with feral Dragons. Wild is wild and should be kept that way. It ensures their survival.

PLANTING FOR DRAGONS

TAIGA/ SUBTUNDRA	TEMPERATE	SUBTROPICAL/ TROPICAL	DESERT
BLACK SPRUCE	SMOKE TREES	MONKEY PUZZLE	TUNA TREES
RED CEDAR	COPPER LEAVES	FLAME TREES	SAGUARO
ROWAN	FERNS/ BRACKEN	DRAGON TREES	DATE PALMS
LARCH	HONEY LOCUST	(NATCH!)	SPINY SMOKE TREES
BIRCH	BEECH	CACAO	BOTTLE TREES
MOSS & LICHENS	HARDY FRUITS	CITRUS TREES	(ANTI- DROUGHT AID)
(VERY HEALTHY)	(APPLE, PEAR, ETC.)	BUTTERFLY BUSHES	ACACIA
BILBERRIES	NINEBARK	BAMBOO	OLIVE
CLOUDBERRIES	SERVICEBERRY	JACARANDA	JOSHUA TREES
(YUM!)	(LOVELY & FRUITY)	CYPRESS	CHASTE TREES

Hardy as the year is long, Dragons usually prefer to crash beneath the stars. Still, when lightning opens the heavens or the summer sun beats down relentlessly, a little shelter from the elements is welcomed by even the most stubborn flier. A rustic lean-to or cliff overhang will often suffice, or if you're good with trees, perhaps a leafy bower is more your style. You'll also want to set up a couple of charming stones and a salt block. Keep it simple

chapter seven

and sturdy, with room for a brace or two to nestle close. (Large as they are, it's amazing how tight Dragons can snuggle when they want to.)

When everything is ready, step back and wait. It may take months or even years, but one day, around dusk, you'll look out and see a Dragon swooping down to your north forty. Once one Dragon lands, others will follow. We don't know how word spreads, but it does; soon your lay-by will be part of a vast global nexus.

A final note: People new to the way of Dragons worry about the hazards of unrelated Dragons sharing the same lay-by. Understandable, but not necessary. The rule of *pax loci*—peace of the place—applies to all visiting Dragons, regardless of origin or species. That said, don't trust it to extend to you and yours. Keep a safe, respectful distance, use the common sense you were born with, and all should be well. And who knows... in time, with individuals who return again and again, you may be able to establish an amicable accord. Don't let your enthusiasm get the better of you, though. Dragons get the first move. Always.

Dragon Keeping

Any Dragon lover will tell you (usually at great length and over a bowl of mulled claret), that nothing in the

world is as satisfying or as exhilarating as being a Dragon keeper. And they would be right.

Dragon keeping is an illustrious art first mentioned in the lore of third-millennium BCE China. During the legendary reign of Shun, last of the Five Emperors, lived a man named Tung Fu, who understood Dragons better than anyone in the empire. Honored by the Emperor as Tung Huan-long—Tung, the Dragon-rearer—he and generations of Huan-longs after him took in Dragons, orphaned, injured, or simply in need of a safe place to crash, and tended each according to their needs, with love and skill. In return, they deigned to power the Emperor's chariot through the skies. This was the birth of Dragon keeping.

Of course, this was China, where Dragons are honored, even venerated. In other parts of the world, not so much. Early Dragon keeping in Europe and the New World was often restricted to a handful of shamans, wizards, and isolated dracophiles. In Europe, the animosity toward our friends meant their guardians had to keep their activities and their charges under wraps. The possibility of torches and pitchforks, not to mention swords and spears, would be an understandable deterrent to even the most ardent Dragon lover.

Over the past two hundred years, as human appreciation of Dragons has grown, so has the interest in Dragon keeping. Unfortunately, this has its downside too. The demand today for eggs and hatchlings far outstrips legitimate supply, which has led to an increase in poaching and subsequent black-market activities. Unregistered hatchlings, for example, mean that somewhere out there, there are Dragon parents, at least, forlorn, at worst, dead. For that reason, there are strict regulations on the breeding and purchase/possession of eggs and Dragonlets. This includes the one-in-a-million occasion when a clutch or orphan is discovered abandoned in the wild: if this happens, call your local Dragon authority at once to register your find. Anyone who objects to such rules shouldn't be around Dragons in the first place.

The same is true of anyone who wants to get into Dragon keeping because they consider it the latest trend in pet ownership and want to be the envy of all their social-media friends. This sort of thinking is at odds with the heart and soul of Dragon keeping. Dragons are no one's flavor of the month; they are not pets—and they will never, ever be "owned." They are, however, dropdead extraordinary, and as such require expert, full-time, multi-generational commitments. The fact is that

> The fact is that as much as people love Dragons and love the *idea* of Dragons, almost all of us are fundamentally unsuited to being Dragon keepers. And that's OK.

as much as people love Dragons and love the *idea* of Dragons, almost all of us are fundamentally unsuited to being Dragon keepers. And that's OK. If you understand that, we can proceed.

First things first: get your papers in order. All Dragon keepers need to be licensed for their protection and that of their charges. You never know when someone might want to make a fuss about a lost cockapoo or avenues of broken corn stalks. Even in our relatively enlightened age, when things go wrong there remains a reflexive tendency to blame the Dragon. Official documents and an abundance of civility can help ease awkward encounters. Also, up your insurance: medical, liability, and fire. Especially fire. You might also want to update your will ... just in case.

With i's dotted and t's crossed, you next want to look to space. Many Dragon keepers started out as overseers of lay-bys, with good reason. Basic requirements are similar—

food, water, shelter—only more so. Now you're essentially creating a human-made weyr with everything from hatching kiln (capable of holding a mature egg and reaching an internal temperature of 2,000° F) to fire quarry, from gliding heights to bathing bowl. Lean-to or overhang may work for transient guests, but for the long-term you'll need a proper Dragon lair that is large, solid, and secure. In terms of food and water, you're not just providing the occasional fly-in with a nosh; instead you are seeing to it that your charge is fed in proper quantity and quality every day of her life. A hundred acres of woods and lake or ocean access are essential. You'll also need land for crops, bees (Dragonlets love honey), and herds of ostrich (hatchlings thrive on ostrich eggs), and a substantial garden for medicinal herbs. Everything must be Dragon-sized. Should you lack a horticulturalist's skill, consider making arrangements with neighborhood farmers, perhaps exchanging nutrient-rich Dragon dung for cart-loads of veggies.

Given the obvious physical and financial demands of this glorious enterprise, it makes sense for several keepers to pool their resources and form communities or Dragon estates. Joining forces and abilities allows you to create an environment fit for a passel of healthy, happy

Dragons. Let's face it, we're not all Rothschilds or Vanderbilts; and the adage that "it takes a village" isn't just for humans.

The fact is, whether starting with an orphan or a hatchling still egg-mucky behind the ears, being a Dragon keeper is, in essence, a matter of serving *in loco dracones*. Standing in for Queen, Sire, and extended enchantment family, a DK is responsible not only for their little one's creature comforts, years of companionship and well-being, but also for teaching their Dragon how to be a Dragon. This is where Dragon estates can be a real blessing. No matter how dedicated or experienced a keeper is, no one can raise a Dragon quite like their own.

Now that you are all set up, how do you acquire a Dragon? Eggs and orphans are the usual way with youngsters, inheritance with older Dragons. Though there are tales of clutches discovered lying about the wilderness, such treasures are as likely to be found as grunions in the Sea of Tranquility. (Not that fortune hunters and poachers don't keep looking.) An exchange among reputable keepers is the only moral way to get eggs. It is also the one way to be sure of your Dragon's lineage. Of course, once estate Dragons reach maturity, they will handle the next generation all by themselves. And your partner will

finally be able to convert the hatching oven into that pottery kiln she's been talking about.

Being even more closely protected than pandas, Chinese Dragons are almost never seen, let alone kept, west of the Gobi or east of the Pacific Rim, or they weren't until recently. The Chinese government has been working with a handful of western Dragon keepers (unfortunately, not yet in the US) on draco-diplomatic exchanges of eggs and occasionally, breeding pairs. This does not always sit well with Dragons, East or West. While they appreciate the idea of being a part of any global rapprochement, not to mention seeing new places and meeting new Dragons, they prefer statesmanship on their own terms. Being used as pawns in human affairs, no matter how noble the cause, does not please. At the very least, they expect to be asked. So, if you find yourself in the midst of an international egg swap, even if it involves the Hwan-lung Minister of Dragons himself, be doubly sure all parties—especially the Dragons—are in accord. After all, the point of diplomacy is to build bridges, not burn them down. With the luck of Great Lung and the blessings of our better angels, Asian Dragons will be found around the globe in a matter of decades.

Whether long-term or short, fostering orphans (aka Dragon rescues) is another way to add to your draconic family. Wars, strip mines, felled forests, fouled seas, hunters: dangers abound in the modern world. Especially in war zones. Dragons do their best, but there are still casualties and hatchlings left behind. This is where WAFDE and the IDC step in. They try to place the little ones where they can get the special care they need and, if it is their wish, be returned to the wild.

Orphans are not for first-time keepers. They are victims of trauma, sometimes physical, always emotional. This frequently creates issues with trust, abandonment, and safety that require an expert hand. If you find yourself tending to a foundling, remember that people have likely been the villains in their young lives. This can make them fearful and/or aggressive at first. Give them their own space where they feel warm, safe, and protected. The presence of other Dragons can help immensely, teaching the little ones by example and observation that you are not the enemy. Until they understand this, caution is the better part of valor … and the best way to keep you out of the hospital.

On the flip side are those Dragonlets who look at their new two-leg keepers as surrogates for the family they lost. They become clingy as a (very large) puppy, sticking close to your heels, even having trouble eating and sleeping alone. Again, the company of other Dragons can be very helpful here, and in extreme cases, the services of a good Dragon behaviorist. With time, love, and care, most orphans outgrow the worst of their trauma symptoms. However, chances are that those with severe abandonment issues will never make it back in the wild, so be sure you have long-term room for one more.

Now and then, no matter how devoted you are to your charges, a dark pall will descend upon them and refuse to go away. This is what we call weyrsickness, or Dragon despondency, and it has been a part of Dragon lore since the beginning. Though any hatchling can be afflicted, the early losses experienced by orphans make them particularly vulnerable. Symptoms to watch out for include loss of appetite, insomnia, nightmares, and a general disinterest in life. We're talking a Dragon-sized case of the Blue Devils. Being an ailment of the spirit, there is no quick and easy cure. Start by using basic Dragon-keeper common

sense: spend as much time with your hatchling as you can, talk to her, play music, even join her in her lair if it comforts her; use toys and games to get her out of herself; introduce her to other creatures—dogs, goats, chinchillas (they love playing with chinchillas, go figure)—other Dragons, if possible. You may not snap her out of her melancholy, but simply giving her a secure space in which to sort things out can work wonders. Should her symptoms linger past weaning, contact a professional. Despite doing everything right, it's possible your little rescue is developing a chronic condition; moving her to an orphan rehab facility might be the best thing for her.

Weyrsickness Remedy

In a 100-gallon copper vat, place:

- 1 hundredweight crushed bittersweet berries
- 40 pounds honey (clover or wildflower preferred)
- 14 pounds forget-me-not petals (or 1 quart of their extract)

Fill the vat with fresh spring water and bring to a boil. Simmer uncovered for 8 hours. Let cool, then decant into 10-gallon kegs.

At the first sign of depression, administer twice daily, 1 pint/each 100 pounds body weight, in your Dragon's food. If desolation persists, double the dosage and consult your cryptoveterinarian as soon as possible.

So your hatchling is now weaned. Pour yourself a tall glass of lemonade (or something stronger) and pat yourself on the back: you both made it. Now get back to work. Your Dragon is growing and that means she's hungry.

It is often said that the way to a Dragon's heart is across her palate, and, in their first couple of years, young Dragons will eat four to eight times a day. What a great opportunity for dietary experimentation! Though large quantities of animal protein are necessary, the choices are fairly routine: fowl, rabbit, deer, fish, occasionally bison, bovine, or antelope. [Note: Family pets and other four-legged acquaintances are, of course, off the menu; if your little one needs more than the game she can catch on her own, consider outsourcing her needs to a nearby ranch. It's easier on everyone.] Fruits and veggies are another story, presenting Dragonlets with a veritable cornucopia of possibilities. Offer your weanling a sumptuous spread with color, texture, and lots of spice, then let her loose. Time and variety are all it takes for her to discover just what tickles her culinary fancy. Fortunately, even at a young age, most Dragons are tuned in to their physical needs. As a rule, they'll avoid overindulging in the empty calories of grains and sweets, preferring to strike a healthy balance between greens and roots rich in calcium and keratin (for scales), and juicy, vitamin C-laden fruits they usually save for afters. Should they err in their dining habits, a large draft of snapdragon tea with honey followed by two days on a bland diet of poultry and orchard grass should set them right. Chances are they will learn from the experience and not repeat it.

Growth means molting, and young Dragons, like young snakes, will shed their skins every three or four weeks. They come through the other side with lustrous scales and room to grow. The molt itself is an excellent insulator and can be used to fill cracks in nests and lairs. Though this is a natural process, they occasionally need a little help, starting with a warm bath and a gentle scrub. New scales are tender, so be sure to have a batch of Molting Balm on hand, and use liberally.

Molting Balm

In a 50-gallon copper cauldron, melt:

20 pounds cocoa butter

20 pounds almond oil

8 pounds of beeswax [Proportions of balm softeners (oils) to balm hardener (wax) may vary depending on how hot or cold your Dragon's temperature runs. Tinker with the proportions until you have a compound right for your Dragon, one which applies with a minimum of elbow grease; excessive rubbing makes for a very unhappy hatchling.]

Add to the mixture:

10 pounds bruised lavender

10 pounds pot marigold (*Calendula officinalis*) [Be sure to harvest the calendula at noon under a bright, hot sun for peak potency.]

2 quarts lemon oil

8 ounces ylang-ylang

Simmer for at least 4 hours, then strain the solids and decant the balm into oaken firkins to cool and solidify. You can also press the herbal residue to extract residual

TIP 8

✦

Dragon Body Language

Though Dragonish is an esoteric language, basic pos-
turing is practically universal. Dragons are often slow to
anger and always aware of their power. Surprise one,
however, and they will flash their neck furls and rat-
tle their scales: "Give me space!" If that's not enough,
they'll puff themselves up, spread their wings, and snarl
to say "Back off!" When in defense of their enchantment, all bets are off. Tails thump the ground, claws rip
the soil, and smoke pours from nostrils—"*Run or burn!*"

On the welcoming side, Eastern Dragons bob their
heads, fluff whiskers, and offer cryptic smiles. Western
Dragons purr when rubbed right behind the ears ... but
make sure you're invited before doing so.

oils. They are both aromatic and efficacious in treating minor wounds and scrapes.

Slather your Dragon with balm immediately after shedding. While always soothing, it is virtually essential in tropical and sub-tropical climes where the risk of sunburn is high. (It works for humans, too.)

As much as Dragons admire strength, they can be extremely stubborn or even contrary in their early years and will challenge even the most experienced Dragon keeper. What's needed are clear rules and a firm hand. If you're working with others, be sure you are all on the same page. It's hard enough growing up Dragon in a human world without getting mixed signals. This is particularly necessary as they enter their troublesome twos and spectacular threes, when given half a chance, they will try to push your buttons and test your authority—don't let them. Bad habits acquired at a young age are almost impossible to break later, not to mention being potentially dangerous. For example, in chapter 3 we discussed the necessary precautions around Dragons learning to breathe fire. Those first licks of flame are exhilarating, yet the perils are very real. For everyone's

sake, be strict but kind and you should come through the experience in one unsinged piece.

Spectacular as Dragon pyrotechnics are, nothing compares to flight. Seeing the world from the back of a soaring Dragon is the stuff a keeper's dreams are made of. First, wings must be spread and aeronautic skills gained. Though a largely instinctual activity, Dragons won't snort and chuff at their person for grabbing a burnishing stone and rubbing the baby velvet from their wings. Bonds are reinforced and an excellent upper-body workout is had. Just be careful not to tear your rotator cuffs.

Every so often, less often than not, a Dragon has trouble getting airborne. Time to dig into your medicine chest and retrieve a bottle of flying ointment (see recipe). Use as directed, and your Dragon should be flying in no time.

Much as you may want to join your charge aloft, it is important to remember that not all Dragons consent to be ridden. Always ask, never presume. And be sure they're experienced on the wing and big enough to carry you. Many keepers give their Dragons a full year or two of solo flight before even approaching them for a lift. If you have taken your time and established an affectionate, respectful connection, you should be able to anticipate many years of flying together, seeing new sights, and

visiting new estates and weyrs. Just remember to dress warm; it gets cold up in the clouds.

Flying Ointment

Less an ointment and more an intense herbal concentrate, flying ointment is potent stuff that must be prepared and handled with care.

Infuse in 2 gallons of cold spring water:

3 quarts foxglove blooms (*Digitalis purpurea*)

2 quarts windflower (*Anemone*) [Gather the windflower in the spring when the blooms are just coming out. Dry or fresh *Anemone* can be used, but remember the dried are more concentrated: use only 1 $^1/_2$ quarts of dried blooms.]

1 pound mugwort (*Artemesia vulgaris*)

Let stand for 12 hours in the sun, then distill, slowly. You should wind up with approximately 1 quart of concentrated essence.

Add to this:

3 ounces Basil Oil (Witches' Herb)

Stir gently—*never shake!*—and decant to an airtight brown glass bottle (dark green if you must). Age in a cool place (basements are good, caves are better) for at least three months. As needed, mix one (1) ounce of concentrate with one (1) gallon of spring water in a large hydro pump. Spray your Dragon's wings—top and bottom—twenty minutes before flying exercises. Do not use for more than ten days, as it has a cumulative effect and can rapidly become too much for a young Dragon to handle.

Remember: when using flying ointment, first, last, and always DILUTE. Dragon lore is replete with cautionary tales, including one of a young Black Forest keeper who forgot this very simple rule. In his eagerness to get his Dragon flying, he treated her wings with full-strength FO and she skyrocketed straight into the firmament. Three days later, when she finally returned to earth, she was definitely not amused. "Schwach oder Sterben!" she roared. *Dilute or die!* Her keeper never forgot again.

Time with a young Dragon is full of wonders large and small, from sharing a sheaf of Naming Day celebrations to more bauble gifting than you can count. (Dragons

love adding baubles to their collections, regardless of the occasion.) There will be regular trips to the farrier for claw trims, and wellness checks with your vet. Your biggest concern will be boredom and the mischief that often comes with it. Remember: Dragons have an innate inclination towards roguery, and juveniles can be real troublemakers. It isn't much of a problem in the wild where survival takes up the Dragon's share of their days, but kept Dragons are a different story. They have a lot more time on their claws, and while we like to say there is no such thing as a bad Dragon, idlers can create problems with the neighbors. A little structured activity is the surest way to engage minds and bodies and guard against ennui. Keep your charges busy with travel and games; encourage them to chip in around the estate, especially with some of the heavy lifting. After some initial grumbling, their pride will start to kick in and they'll be increasingly happy to help. Freeloading is just not the Dragon way.

Time with a young Dragon is full of wonders large and small.

They understand TANSTAAFL in their bones, and it gets them far.

For the next twenty-five or thirty years, you will grow together, and together you'll know joys and sorrows, midnight songs and midsummer Dragon tales. The decades will simply fly by. Then, one day, without even realizing it, you run smack into the next monumental milestone: your Dragon has reached sexual maturity.

For those so inclined, it is time to find a mate. Watch for mood changes, and be sure their circle of friends, acquaintances, and potential partners is large enough that they don't have to settle or fly wild. If your Dragon pairs up beyond the estate's bounds, be sure to work out the logistics of who lives where, especially if there are plans for little ones in the future. Other than that, there's not much for you to do. Dragons mix and match, hopefully without too many spats or hurt feelings, and handle all the personal details. Just be supportive and show up for the festivities. There must always be festivities. If it suits the pair—and pleases the Great Dragon—the scrabble of little Dragon feet may be heard up and down your estate in the not-too-distant future. Plan accordingly. (And, yes, there will be bigger, better, more splendidly draconic celebrations for the occasion.)

So the years pass, unremarkably remarkable. But there is a final leg in the Dragon keeper's journey, one filled with wills, legacies, and saying good-bye.

There was a reason understood way back in the time of Tung Huan-long that Dragon keeping was a family affair: Dragons outlive us. As it is 99.9 percent probable that you will die before your scaly companion, be sure to take her into account when hashing things out with your lawyers and estate planners. Above all, include your Dragon in these discussions. It may be your death, but it's her life— it's only right to ask her how she wants to live it.

Acutely aware of the laws of nature, most Dragons adjust to the passing of their keepers, accepting that their care has been handed to the next generation, to children now grown who once played with them when they were mere hatchlings. They are taller now, perhaps graying round the temples, but if they have learned the ways of Dragon keepers, they will do. Some Dragons are very much one-person creatures. No matter how generous or caring their extended human family, they find home without their person too empty and painful to bear. They are apt to fly free or to dwell around the fringes of their former home, visiting now and then like a distant cousin who drops in for holidays and family reunions. Still others

may not know how the loss of their person will affect them until it actually happens, so daughters and sons, attend: much as you love them, you can't keep Dragons who won't be kept.

It is orphans who give aging keepers the most concern, those Dragons who, when young, latched onto their humans for dear life and never learned how to let go. Chances are that they will not survive in the wild and so must be provided for with the utmost care. Do not wait 'til the last minute. When the morning cold starts seeping into your bones, it's time to take your Dragon aside, to begin easing her into good-byes. If she's not close to other members of your family or estate (or if you are a solo keeper and so have no family or estate), your task will be harder. Start by introducing her to the best keepers you know, those with a gentle hand, lots of patience, and other Dragons. Give them time, and don't hesitate to consult a professional as needed.

With great care and a draconic dose of luck, the transition will be sad but smooth when the time comes. Until then, spend time together, take long walks, gentle flights, tell stories, and sing songs. In short, do the things you both enjoy. There is no better way to honor the years you've shared. And as dusk bleeds into night, you'll be able to say, as did Ged in Ursula K. Le Guin's *The Farthest Shore*, "I do not care what comes after; I have seen the dragons on the wind of morning" (Le Guin, 1972).

Now, I want to close this chapter with a little timeless wisdom from the early years of modern Dragon keeping. At the beginning of the twentieth century, Dr. Amelia Penrhyn-Haile, cryptoherpetologist and Dragon keeper extraordinaire, had the prescience to set down a decalogue for future Dragon keepers. Much to enchantment chagrin, her words have been updated over the years and trimmed of their Edwardian formality, but their import remains. All Dragon keepers should have a copy of Dr. Amelia's words writ large and posted prominently.

Covenant of the Dragon Keeper

1. This above all things is true: They are Dragons. *All* Dragons are wild.

2. Love your Dragon as yourself; treat her always with kindness and affection, and respect her choices in life and love, present and future.

3. Never give your Dragon a silly—i.e., human—name. She will only laugh in your face and singe your eyebrows.

4. When your Dragon speaks, listen.

5. Always keep your Dragon mentally stimulated and physically fit. Boredom leads to misery. Misery breeds mischief.

6. Never have fire practice near the house, woods, or during droughts.

7. Honor your Dragon's Remembrance-of-Name Day; celebrate always with proper Dragonish feasting and flair.

8. Never use a saddle or a bridle when flying with your Dragon.

9. Teach your Dragon proper etiquette, especially with regard to neighbors, pets, livestock, and fields. No buzzing; no eating; no scorching. Courtesy counts.

10. First roar to last, this is the commitment and responsibility of a Dragon keeper. We are talking centuries. Always be open with your Dragon about life's impending changes, sharing fears, needs, and options. Provide for her care after your passing. Or, if it is her wish, give her your blessing as she flies free.

Chapter Eight

ROUGHING IT: DRAGON-WATCHING IN THE WILD

S o, that thousand-acre parcel for your Dragon estate will break your bank, and your zoning board won't approve the lay-by you propose for the old golf course. What is a Dragon lover to do? Where and how do you find Dragons in the wild?

First, pack a bag. You're hitting the road. While draco-philes use modern technology as enthusiastically as the next person, when it comes to going into the wilderness, many of us remain Luddites at heart. GPS and digital maps have their place, but in Dragon country nothing

serves like a proper hard-bound atlas. Better yet, switch to detailed topographical maps and a reliable compass when on foot. They won't let you down.

Next, contact your local Dragon authorities and work out a fitting itinerary. This is where the resources of WAFDE and the International Dragon Conservancy are invaluable. According to the most recent Dragon census, there are seventy-four registered weyrs in the world. Some are isolated by geography or shifting political circumstance. Still others are under strict "Keep Out!" regulations for the safety of Dragons and people alike. There are approximately thirty weyrs and surrounding sanctuary lands one can visit, and a half dozen more one can get close enough to for chance Dragon sightings. After all, borders are nothing but artificial human constructs to our scaly friends. In the end, Dragons will fly where they choose.

Though parts of Asia and Latin America are slowly opening up for draco-tourism, the most accessible weyrs are currently in Canada, the United States, and Europe. Their relatively stable societies combine with strong Dragon traditions and conservation efforts to provide spaces where Dragons can simply be Dragons and we humans can experience their wonder.

There are four basic Dragon habitats in the world: mountains, upland forests, lowlands, and deserts. They overlap, of course—desert mountains, lowland forests— with coastal habitats absorbed into the dominant environs at hand. Once familiar with them and the particular Dragons they support, let your personal preferences rule and plan your adventures accordingly. After all, we all have our favorite spots, where the primal forces of Earth and Dragon come together and speak to us. Arid deserts or cool mountain forests, inland moors or rugged shores— if you are willing to stray from the beaten path, there are Dragons out there just waiting. (And hoping that their homes don't vanish beneath rising seas, lumbered jungles, or concrete plains—but that is a discussion for another time.) And remember: no matter where you go, these are wilderness experiences up close and personal. Even when Dragons stay out of sight, as is occasionally

> Arid deserts or cool mountain forests, inland moors or rugged shores—if you are willing to stray from the beaten path, there are Dragons out there, just waiting.

their wont, the diversity of indigenous flora and fauna you'll encounter makes every journey exceptional.

For now, let's start at the top.

Mountains

The human penchant for settling relatively flat, arable lands has left the higher, rockier terrains to pica and ibex, eagle and snow leopard. And, of course, Dragons. As our cities spread and sprawled below, Dragons around the world retreated to the peace and safety of higher elevations. From the Himalayas to the Andes, Rockies to Alps, they roared atop sun-drenched mountains and nested deep in stalagmited chambers when the hurricane-force winds of winter blew.

Above the tree line, where thin air and barren crags are the norm, some of the hardiest Dragons in the world make their homes. Like their Polar cousins, mountain Dragons are shaggy around the edges. They retain their hatchling fur for warmth and have wide, snowshoe-like paws that keep them from crashing through freshly fallen powder. They charm their horns to fine points on the bare rocks, take bracing dips in glacier-fed tarns, and have fire practice without fear of igniting the landscape.

The lack of vegetation also means they're strictly carnivorous for a good nine months out of the year, with

sure-footed goats and sheep and the occasional marmot making up the bulk of their diet. Deep caves and mountain cold allow an enchantment to fill their weyr larders in anticipation of lean winter days, and though Dragons don't literally hibernate, they are able to slow their metabolisms to preserve energy, if need be. Unfortunately, all those months without fresh greens and the vitamins that come with them often leads to softening and/or cracking of the scales. Come spring, Dragons are weary of one-note dining. They eagerly spread their wings, catch a rising thermal, and sail below the tree line to eat shoots and leaves. This green feast improves both their scales and their temperaments and prepares them for the busy months ahead.

Unless you are an intrepid mountaineer, the best time and place to experience the majesty of mountain Dragons is late May to early August (November to February in southern heights), in the verdant alpine and semi-alpine foothills. It is also the safest. You can watch them soar and swoop without risk of frostbite or tumbling into a crevasse. And, should a Dragon sing, as well they might, an avalanche won't come roaring down on your head.

So, with all the mountains in the world, where do you go? It is said of alpine enchantments, "Pick a peak and

chapter eight
191

you'll find a Dragon." Hyperbolic though it sounds, the Himalayan Quad is the one place on Earth where it's close to being true. Situated near the Roof of the World, this is a Dragon-rich region that supports four weyrs, possibly more, the oldest of which is Kang Rinpoche Weyr in the sacred shade of Mount Kailash.

Centuries of isolation, not to mention intense surges of ley energy, made for strong, savvy Dragons who flew through passes and over summits from Kashmir to Bhutan and round the edge of the Tibetan Plateau. They capered from the headwaters of the Ganges to the shores of Nam Co. Sadly, since the Sino-Tibetan conflicts of the 1950s and the ongoing skirmishes between India and Pakistan, they have become much more circumspect.

The Dragons have also been dispirited by the increasing number of mountaineers who see their home range as the last great challenge to human chutzpah and frailty. The litter on Everest, K-2, and the Annapurna Massif is enough to break the heart of the bravest Dragon. (Imagine if one of their kind did that to your home!) If you are a climber and insist upon venturing close, remember this: Mountain Dragons treasure their pristine, unpeopled world and will protect it fiercely if they must. As a basic rule of thumb, if you can't breathe the air on your own, stick to lower alti-

tudes. Given recent political and ecological tensions, Quad Dragons are best experienced from afar, in the foothills of northern India and Nepal.

You might have better luck encountering mountain Dragons further west: Porcupine River Weyr in the Ogilvie Mountains of Canada's Yukon Territory; Tonrar Pass in Denali National Park, Alaska; Vientos Emplumados in the Andes; and Harunu Weyr in New Zealand's South Island Alps. (Yes, not all Kiwi Dragons are Peter Jackson CGI creations.)

What about the European Alps, you ask? Centuries of bloody conflict, topped by two devastating world wars in thirty years, and, more recently, climate change, have wreaked havoc on the Alpine weyrs. During WWI, for example, Draghi Marmolada Weyr in the Dolomites became a high-altitude nexus for both Italian and Austro-Hungarian forces. Dragons are not fools—in the face of modern weaponry, they chose to abandon their home, leaving enchantment chambers to frostbitten troops and pearly glaciers to stains of human blood. Today, few remember what the battles were about, but the loss of the Dragons has been and will be felt for generations.

Upland Forests

Though European mountain Dragons are few and far between, the same cannot be said of the continent's upland forest Dragons. Down from rocky summits, where the trees grow thick as Merlin's beard, Dragons live in abundance. The upland forests of the world have everything a Dragon could want: plentiful and varied food, sweet water, and shelter, either ready-made or easily excavated. In fact, temperatures are moderate enough that many a Dragon will eschew shelter altogether and simply rough it under the stars for most of the year.

The woodlands of Europe and North America, the wilds of Manchuria, the treed hills of Peru, and the eerie highland tepui of Venezuela are all areas that fit upland Dragons to a T. With vegetation rich in nutrients, prey ranging in size from vole to bison, and lakes and rivers jumping with fish, the ingredients for joyful enchantment living are all around. True, they share the land with other large predators—bears, catamounts, wolverines—but the land is bountiful; there is food enough for all. The biggest threats to weyr existence are of human origin: clear-cut lumbering, mining, hunting, and recreational use.

Despite the abundance of food and space, upland Dragons are smaller than their mountain kin. Dwarfed

by the closeness of tree and shrub, they're able to move about without disturbing their woodland neighbors or leaving obvious Dragon signs. This is particularly true of southern Feathered Dragons, who are agile enough to navigate through kapok and jacaranda without cracking a twig or spooking their simian prey. They are also very cautious when it comes to their fire, especially in the dry season. Though conifers can handle considerable lack of rainfall, their resinous sap is highly flammable at the best of times. To guard against their home going up like flash paper, an upland weyr will often clear a stone ledge for fire practice, a good indication Dragons are about. And though usually sporting an array of greenish/brownish scales to blend into their environs, they will also leave strategically placed stands of tree round their weyrs to hide them from prying—or casual—eyes.

Until recently, the upland forests were considered almost as safe for Dragons as the mountains. Aside from the occasional hiker or trapper, human sightings were as rare as piranha in Lake Champlain. In the late nineteenth century, the occasional became the persistent; lumber barons and mining magnates moved in and started ravaging the environment. When Teddy Roosevelt and the Boone and Crockett Club sought to preserve public

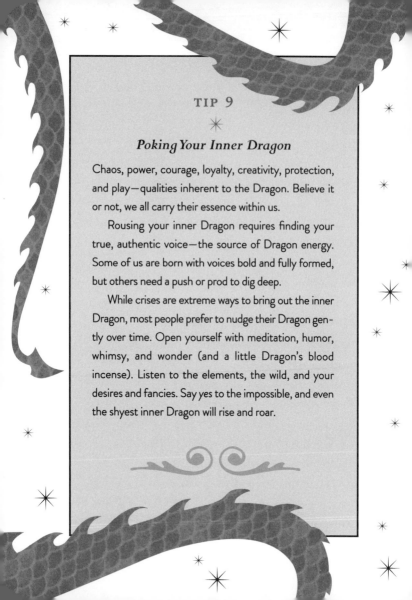

TIP 9

✴

Poking Your Inner Dragon

Chaos, power, courage, loyalty, creativity, protection, and play—qualities inherent to the Dragon. Believe it or not, we all carry their essence within us.

Rousing your inner Dragon requires finding your true, authentic voice—the source of Dragon energy. Some of us are born with voices bold and fully formed, but others need a push or prod to dig deep.

While crises are extreme ways to bring out the inner Dragon, most people prefer to nudge their Dragon gently over time. Open yourself with meditation, humor, whimsy, and wonder (and a little Dragon's blood incense). Listen to the elements, the wild, and your desires and fancies. Say yes to the impossible, and even the shyest inner Dragon will rise and roar.

lands in the United States, they did the Dragons of North America a true solid. As acres of state and national park and forest wilderness were protected, the indigenous species, including Dragons, flourished. Similar conservation programs around the globe have made upland forest weyrs the most numerous Dragon habitats in the world.

If you are up for a hike through the woods, coupled with the marveling at Dragons playing hide and seek with a scurry of squirrels, you have an array of destinations from which to choose. My favorites in the Americas include to the north, Willapa Hills Weyr, south of Seattle in the lush Pacific Northwest; Chilko Lake Weyr in the green hills of central British Columbia; Llyn Carreg near Stone Lake, Ontario, said to have been founded by an enchantment of Welsh Reds, refugees from the Dark Times; and in New England, Katahdin Weyr in the Maine woods and Dragons' Nest, near Glastenbury, Vermont. (The coniferous Greens are ideal for upland Dragons, even though we call them mountains—a distinction that makes mountain Dragons laugh.)

Feathered Dragon lovers will need to go further afield. In the dense forests of Central America there is Ka Hun P'e Che', home to Dragons some say are descended from Sovereign Plumed Serpent herself. Even further south is

K'uycha Phuru Weyr. Situated east of Cuzco at the edge of the Inca's Sacred Valley, its Dragons have been known to tip their wings over Macchu Pichu and have solstice races along the Nazca Lines.

If you're in Europe, you might explore Mentor's Mound, a small weyr in the hills of Ithaca, or Négy Kis Sárkány—Weyr of the Four Little Dragons—in the legendary forests of the Carpathian Mountains (there are more than werewolves and vampires in those hills). The British Isles are rich with upland habitats, notably Gwydir Forest Weyr in northwestern Wales (Wales wouldn't be Wales without Dragons!), and, further north, the largest weyr in the UK, Glendhragon. Tucked into Scotland's Cairngorms hills, Glendhragon is not only home to three burgeoning enchantments (at last count), but also in the heart of Highland distillery country. If you fancy a heathery single malt after a day of Dragon watching, you can't go wrong.

These are just a few of the upland forest weyrs dotted around the world. Others, like those in Russia, Ukraine, the African highlands, and remote parts of South America, are not currently considered safe destinations, due to human, not draconic, hostilities. When things settle,

WAFDE is hoping to get back to these places and check on the status of the weyrs.

Unfortunately, war is not the only threat to the upland Dragons. In the States, for example, recent government policies have shifted from generations of conservancy back to exploitation. Public lands—even national monuments and parks—have been opened up to industrial devastation and hunting in moves reminiscent of the worst land grabs of the 1800s. Combine that with climate change denial and weakening of clean air and water protections and trouble looms. For short-term profits, we are putting not only the oft-mentioned spotted owl, grizzly bear, and sage grouse at risk, but also lynx, stone marten, and Dragon. While administrations come and go— and hopefully, their myopic policies with them—many of us are currently relying on the kindness of private conservation-minded strangers to secure thousands of acres against mining, drilling, and deforestation. Such ventures are a lifeline for Dragons and their fellow forest denizens.

A few closing words to the wisely adventurous: Stick with your guide at all times. And if you are camping in the upland forests, don't count on a bear bag to keep your supplies safe from young Dragons. They are smart,

mischievous, and can get into anything, no matter how high it's hung in a tree.

Lowlands

Long, long ago, the lowlands of the world were awash with Dragons. It made sense: these were areas surrounding lakes, rivers, gentle plains, and ancient deciduous forests—prime real estate. There was prey aplenty and enough room for the largest Dragons to spread their wings. Back then, the lowland Dragons were giants among giants, hobnobbing with the other megafauna from steppe to coastal delta. Then, around 8,000 years ago, humans began shedding their nomadic ways, building villages and cities, planting crops where once only shrubs and wild grasses grew.

To make room for such two-legged expansion, old forests were felled and plains plowed. Rivers were no longer for swimming and Dragon-play but navigated for trade and diverted for irrigation. Needless to say, the interests of Dragons and encroaching humans were on a collision course. One has only to recall the tale of St. George, who slew a Dragon at odds with the people of Cappadocia over an issue of water rights. Of course, Cappadocia's in the arid plains of central Anatolia and the Dragon was there first. It was a conflict waiting to happen.

In the end, Dragons were driven out, and humans claimed virtually all the lowlands in temperate and tropical realms. Though surviving in the occasional place name or scarred knoll, the Dragons of yore are today mere spectral visions from history and legend. Their once-majestic weyrs have been buried beneath cities from London to Montreal, Buenos Aires to Kiev, their steppe earthworks worn flat beneath the hooves of Mongol hordes.

Most displaced Dragons assimilated into upland forest enchantments, yet those who fancied cooler climates went north to the taiga plains of Eurasia and Canada, where the paucity of humans made them feel safe. There, among musk ox and ptarmigan, they shaped earth and snow into nesting chambers and hunted alongside bears and wolves. Though they have adapted over time, the sight of Dragons thundering about Baffin Island and Nunavut's Arctic coast can't help but make one think of kinder days and wonder if those same Dragons might not prefer basking on more temperate plains.

Wild lowland Dragons may be nearly impossible to find today, but that doesn't mean you won't see them dipping and diving over field and plain. Thanks to the renaissance in Dragon keeping, our scaly friends have returned to more populated areas of the world . . . and it's probably best this way. Where wild Dragons may willfully challenge the conventions of human society, Dragons who have grown up around us understand their purpose, so accidents are less likely to happen ... a good thing for all concerned. Still, for safety's sake, don't blithely approach a Dragon on the village green unless you know her personally.

Deserts

Of all the habitats in the world, deserts are least hospitable to Dragons. Too much sand and blistering sun; too little water and cooling shade, not to mention the lack of quantity and diversity of food for such large creatures. In short, while Dragons can be found in deserts, they are rare, and rather hostile, like their environs. Competition for resources is fierce, and they have every intention of coming out on top.

These scrappy, small-scaled Dragons build their weyrs in mesas and cliffsides. Aligned with the prevailing winds, these marvels of design keep even the honeycombed maze of tunnels and chambers naturally air-cooled, or as much as is possible. Their metabolisms have adapted to the point where they need minimal water and remarkably little food (one major meal per fortnight usually suffices). Easily the most ectothermic of Dragons, their scales absorb heat during the day like solar panels and keep them going through the cold desert nights. They are also experts at camouflage, using their tawny scales and otherworldly stillness to morph into angular "dunes" or curious "boulders" adrift on an ocean of sand.

Once upon a time, desert Dragons were seen from the dunes of the Namib to the wadi near Timbuktu, from West African ergs to the arid dasht of eastern Persia. They would race among the red cliffs of Petra and find respite in the waters of the Euphrates. In the New World, they romped from one side of the Rio Grande to another, consorting with the Anasazi and splashing in the shallows of the Salton Sea. But that was all long ago. Note that although Dragons have been reported in the Atacama, dry as the habitat is, these particular high-altitude fliers prefer to be put in the mountain category.

As of our last census, a handful of desert weyrs still survive in the Near East and North Africa, though the exact number of individual Dragons is a mystery. More to the point, they are all under siege. The ravages of two world

Just to be safe, don't blithely approach a Dragon on the village green unless you know her personally.

wars, sectarian violence, the petroleum industry, drought and famine have put already-testy enchantments on high alert. Today, even die-hard desert lovers in the mold of Antoine Saint-Exupéry and Gertrude Bell should think twice ... then twice again ... about visiting the region. Perhaps the situation will change. We hope so. We hope there will be a time when Dragons and humans can again share the hushed beauties and challenges of the desert without fear, a time when we can know, as Saint-Exupéry wrote, that "through the silence something throbs, and gleams" (Saint-Exupéry, *The Little Prince*, 1971).

Chapter Nine
DRAGON FESTIVALS AND FUN

Before the Dark Times, Dragon rites and festivals (of which there were many) were imbued with auras of solemnity and reverence. When shamans danced on sacred ground to summon Dragons, they invoked the most powerful magic at their command. They worshipped Dragons from snout to spade for the fear they inspired and the blessings they bestowed—for their divine magnificence.

The people spoke with the Dragons, learned their songs and dances and festive ways. And when the Dragons left—

When the Dragons left—as Dragons do—the people kept their celebrations, made them their own in joyous memory. Everyone needs some Dragon in their life, if only secondhand.

as Dragons do—the people kept their celebrations and made them their own in joyous memory. They knew that everyone needs some Dragon in their lives, if only second-hand.

Dragons may no longer be seen as gods, but they are still celebrated. East and west, local and global, fun has replaced somber ritual in fetes that honor Dragons or are simply Dragon-friendly. So if you love our friends but prefer them less flesh-and-flame and more painted-and-papier-mâché (I can't imagine why, personally!), leave tent and hiking boots at home and map out an itinerary of Dragon festivals. Plan your travels well, and you can keep to the company of fellow dracophiles *and* fair-hopping Dragons for much of the year.

Dragon Boats from the East

The most colorful and festive draconic revels all seem to have their inception in Asia, where, since time immemorial, people have both treasured Dragons and known how

to appeal to their vanity. It's a weakness Long, Ryu-jin, and their kindred aren't always proud of, but they'll own it. Besides, who wouldn't be flattered by music, dancing, fireworks, and feasting all in one's name? In return, the Dragons tempered the rains, protected rivers and crops, and blessed all people great and small—an equitable exchange.

Of the Eastern festivals, Duanwu, aka the Dragon Boat Festival, is easily the most familiar and ubiquitous of the lot. It spread from southern China to virtually every corner of the globe. Taking place on the fifth day of the fifth lunar month of the Chinese calendar (a day in late May or early June by Gregorian reckoning), Duanwu is a time to honor the power and good fortune of Dragons. It is also a most auspicious day in terms of Chinese numerology—a double fifth, where five is the number of the elements as well as the number associated with the Emperor. Add the luck of Dragons to a double fifth and you are blessed indeed.

Like many Dragon festivals, Duanwu's origins are ancient and varied. Dragons enjoy the oldest genesis story best, of course, which goes something like this:

Once upon a time, many centuries before China was a country as we know it, centuries even before the Spring and Autumn time of Laozi and Confucius, the people along the southern rivers knew well the ways and magic of Dragons. They worshipped the Dragon King, ruler of all things elemental, and his minions who ruled the local waters and falling rains. For their reverence, the people were rewarded with bountiful crops and nets heaving with fish. There was peace and plenty; with the approach of Summer Solstice, the people set aside a day—the fifth of the fifth—to celebrate the Dragons who made it all possible. They made batches of sticky rice dumplings (*longzi*) stuffed with fruit and meat and wrapped in bamboo leaves. Then in their elaborately carved and painted Dragon boats, they raced onto the river and scattered the dumplings on the water: a feast fit for a Dragon. With the offerings made, the people continue on, rowing between villages to visit kith and kin. There were presents, feasts, and the promise of a good season to come.

Over the years, the story of Duanwu was altered to suit the times. The veneration of Dragons was eventually left behind, and it became a day to commemorate patriotic poets and national heroes, lost to the waters and the creatures beneath. As the people of China traveled the world, Duanwu and its beautifully carved Dragon boats traveled with them, becoming almost emblematic of the

melting pot of civilization. Today, it is a largely secular Dragon carnival. There is food (especially lucky dumplings), music, Dragon dances, and, of course, Dragon boat races. Kuala Lumpur, Yokohama, Vancouver, Boston, London, Auckland, San Francisco, Helsinki, Limassol— every spring, on river, lake, and sea, Dragons race for fun and glory and touch the people with the blessings of the Great Long.

Pagan Days and Saints

In Europe's Pagan past, Dragons and Druids gathered to celebrate a plethora of holidays, especially the quarter and cross quarter days that mark the turns of the Wheel of the Year. This tradition continues among today's enchantments and Neopagans. It makes sense, given the Dragons' incredible power and synchronization with the seasons. Festivals associated with fire—Imbolc, Beltane, Lughnasadh, and Samhain—always give Dragons a particular thrill, with Samhain—Halloween—holding a special place in their hearts.

Many of us think of October 31 as a time for mischief and masquerades, jack-o'-lanterns, goblins, and an overindulgence in sweets. For Dragons, Samhain is a more solemn, even sacred time. It is a reminder of the grief and trauma of the Dark Times, of Dragons lost and weyrs torn asunder. It is also a reminder of how in the bloodiest days of the Middle Ages, when Westies had their wings against the wall, the mystical Sidhe came to their rescue, offering European enchantments sanctuary in the Other-world. At faërie invitation, Dragons young and old vanished into the mists, surviving until such time as humanity came to its senses.

Yet, even when the world was at its most hostile, there was one day in the year when the barrier between the realms of Sidhe and human became thin as gossamer: Samhain. No matter how crazy kings and nations were acting, Dragons would return to their old haunts on that one day to dance across the face of the moon (a sight often mistaken for large bats) and play hide-and-seek with the mystically attuned. As night darkened into dawn, a great wail would rise into the heavens, a mourning cry for Dragons lost or left behind ... and then the veil closed, and the Dragons were gone until the next year.

Though enchantment exile ended long ago, Samhain remains a day when the strange and unusual—be they tiny as pillywiggins or immense as Dragons—walk abroad. It is a day of fire and remembrance, of thanksgiving to friends in a time of great need.

On a lighter note, the calendar is littered with lesser-known Pagan celebrations for Dragons and pseudodragons alike. The second Thursday before Yule, for example, is Picrous Day, when digger dragons across Cornwall kick up a storm—as well as a passel of pixies—to commemorate the discovery of tin on the moors; Holy Wells Day (March 2) is sacred to all Dragons whose ancestors once guarded the leys of sacred grove and spring. To this day, where you find people lighting belfires on Beltane or invoking the unseen on Samhain, you will find Dragons and dracophiles in attendance.

With the spread of Christendom, saints and their feast days became all the rage. Some, like Brigid and Walpurga, were barely disguised adaptations of Pagan figures and retained much of their draconic followings. But make no mistake: Paganism was under attack, and Europe celebrated Dragons less and Dragon slayers more as a result: Theodore of Amasea (November 9), Margaret of Antioch (July 20), and Clement of Metz (November 23). And then there are the holy Dragon tamers: Samson of Dol (July 28), Petroc (June 4), Keyne of the Holy Well (October 8), and Romain of Rouen (October 23). A curious aside: many of the latter just happened to be born in the Dragon-loving Welsh hills.

Dragons and their people have also adopted a handful of saints as their own. Most notable are Francis (October 4), for his love of all creatures; Isidore of Seville (April 4), for his curiosity and erudition about the natural world (though they hold him to grievous fault for his views on Judaism); and Æthelthryth (Audrey) of Northumbria, who had a draconic fondness for baubles and bangles. Her annual fairs are thick with trinkets, the perfect place for a person to find a gift for that hard-to-please Dragon.

Then there is St. Martha (July 29) and the dragon of Tarascon, France. The story goes that, after the death of Jesus (circa 48 CE), Martha, Mary, and Lazarus of Bethany left Judea and settled in what is now Provence. Now, there lived in the area a great dragon-creature known as the Tarasque. For generations he'd roamed the woods between Arles and Avignon, minding his own business, as a dragon does. Then came an influx of humans—not to mention Roman legions tramping through Gaul—and his temper soured. He began rampaging across the countryside, devouring herds and flocks, capsizing boats on the Rhône, and generally terrorizing the populace. The people of Tarascon appealed to Martha for aid; armed with only the tools of her faith, she set off to confront the Tarasque and put things right. Using

prayer, holy water, and a cross, she tamed the rage that burned in his belly. Then she draped her sash over his neck, and with nary a hair out of place, escorted him back to Tarascon. Needless to say, jaws dropped and conversions to the new religion went through the roof. Now, every year, the town holds a festival in Martha's name, in which a young saintly stand-in leads an effigy of the Tarasque through the streets. The dragon is also trotted out for various seasonal fetes and guild fairs from Provence to the Iberian Peninsula, his fierce nature now gentled and beneficial.

In fact, as long as they don't frighten the horses, Dragons are welcome most everwhere, even at the Feast of St. George.

Though these saints' days are essentially remnants of the Dark Times, full of Dragons-as-Satan symbolism, thanks to a shift in draconic perception, in recent years the celebrations have become considerably more Dragon-friendly. In fact, as long as they don't frighten the horses, Dragons are welcome most everywhere, even at the Feast of St. George.

Fire, Flight, Feasting, and Song:
A Global Miscellany

If religious pageantry, benign though it might be, gives you Dark Times flashbacks, and Dragon regattas don't float your boat, fear not. There are options we've yet to explore, festivals that, while not exactly Dragon specific, definitely tickle their fancies and welcome them with open arms. These are fetes of fire and flight, feasting and song.

Dragons and fire are a natural fit, and enchantments are delighted when humans around the world celebrate with flames on a draconic scale. Comrie Flambeaux (New Year's Eve) in Perthshire, Scotland, Quema del Diablo (first week in December) in Guatemala, and Wakaku-sayama mountain burn (fourth Saturday in January) in Nara, Japan, to name a few; all have growing numbers of Dragons and dracophiles among their devotees. And what English Dragon doesn't remember the fifth of November?

Then there are the Big Three: Diwali, Burning Man, and Up Helly Aå.

Diwali is the most religious of the trio. Hindu in origin, it is also celebrated by Sikhs, Jains, and the Newar Buddhists of Nepal. For five days around the new moon in the month of Kartika (October-November, in Gregorian terms), hundreds of millions of people come together

for holy days full of lights, feasts, pyrotechnics, and tributes to Lakshmi, goddess of prosperity and good fortune. With candles and fireworks illuminating the night sky, Diwali celebrates the triumph of light over darkness, knowledge over ignorance, and good over evil. Dragons the world over not only approve but are eager to join in.

When Burning Man first lit up Nevada's Black Rock Desert back in the early 1990s, it drew Dragons and their people from across the continent. Rowdy, creative, with an eco-friendly, leave-no-trace ethos, it was a late-summer must on any Dragon keeper's itinerary. Of late, however, despite sporting a Dragon on its website, it has grown too commercial and unwieldy for all save die-hard festival Dragons. The same cannot be said for some of its regional offshoots like AfrikaBurn in Tankwa Karoo, South Africa, Kiwiburn in New Zealand, and Eiru in County Wexford, Ireland. They are smaller and more personal but adhere to the tenets of Burning Man, as welcoming communities for those—skin or scaled—who treasure the burn.

Finally, for those with an affinity for 20+-hour nights punctuated by flames, head to Scotland's remote Shetland Islands. Every year, on the last Tuesday in January, thousands gather in the burgh of Lerwick to mark the end of Yuletide with the spectacular Up Helly Aå. Though its current incarnation stems from a Victorian effort to keep young Shetlanders out of drunken mischief, the celebration's trappings hearken back to the islands' ninth-century Norse colonization: bands of guizers clad as Vikings, Dragon-prowed ships, and fire (lots of it) to beat back the sub-arctic night. At its climax, torch-bearing, historically-costumed residents drag a longship through the town. (60° N latitude though they are, the islands' maritime climate is temperate even in the depths of winter.) With fanfare and flourish, the galley is set alight, burning to ash as the assembled company sing, dance, and carouse until dawn. Lerwick and Up Helly Aå are draconic bliss for sure.

Humans are fascinated with flight, and this, in turn, fascinates Dragons. Unfortunately, Dragons and air-shows don't exactly mix. In barnstorming days, a dozen-plus Dragons whooshing through tail slides and barrel rolls beside bi-planes, though visually stunning, could also create catastrophic wind shear. The effects can be even more disastrous when flying among hot-air balloons—a fact that makes you wonder if a Nebraska Flathorn sent a certain humbug balloonist to Oz rather than an unexpected Omaha updraft. For the protection of all concerned, strict rules were passed in the 1940s that relegated Dragons to the air-show sidelines.

Barred from participation—and not terribly thrilled by the roar of modern jet engines ("Dragons roar, not machines!")—Dragons and their people have turned to quieter and more colorful aerobatic amusements: kite festivals. Dragon kites, long-tailed and broad-winged, have been a staple of such celebrations for centuries, becoming bigger and more remarkable with each generation. You can begin in mid-January with Gujarat, India's International Kite Festival, then head east to Weifang, China in spring, across the Pacific to the Americas for festivals from one coast to the other, from June to September. And that's just the start. Europe has its share of kite fests, too—Bristol, UK; Cervia, Italy; Öland, Sweden; Ede, Netherlands—and Australia, and South America. In short, wherever the wind blows and imaginations soar, there will be kites, many of which look like or are at least inspired by Dragons.

To Dragon eyes, one of the best kite festivals is part of Dragefesten (Dragon Fest) held annually in mid-June in the commune of Sola on Norway's Atlantic coast. Sponsored by the local Drageklubb (Dragon Club), the kite festival is not only Dragon-centric but also cutting-edge, with people coming from around the world to show off their aerodynamic wonders. With windswept cliffs and plenty of fish in the sea, the Sola festival is an exquisite midsummer diversion for Dragons and their people. One caveat before you go: If traveling with young Dragons, remember that they, like kittens, are particularly fond of string play. Manners count—letting them run amok among intricately strung anchors and spars will not only tick off people who've sunk time and passion into their kites but also get you banned from next year's fun.

No discussion of Dragon festivals would be complete without a visit to Wales, home to Y Ddraig Goch, the Red Dragon, not to mention some of the finest poets and musicians in the world. The Welsh know how to celebrate them all. While many a Cymric festival, such as the Dragon Festival in Rhayader on the River Wye, include a Dragon or two, it's the people's respect for the ancient ways of Druid and Celt that really stroke a Dragon's whiskers. Some find this in the holidays linked to the Celtic Wheel and mentioned in the tales of the Mabinogian. And some wait for summer days when, from Anglesey to Mumbles Head, the people of Wales celebrate the

eisteddfodau. These literary and musical gatherings are steeped in the traditions of the Cymry. Traditions shimmering with draconic spirit and flair.

The idea of the eisteddfod dates back, at least, to 1176, when Rhys ap Gruffydd, Prince of South Wales, summoned poets and musicians from across the British Isles to his Christmas Court at Cardigan Castle. Aside from celebrating the literary and euphonious talents of the participants, it was also a way to recognize the peace between Lord Rhys's Wales and Henry II's England, a contentious peace which, sadly, did not outlast the Plantagenet king's death.

Ensuing centuries saw the bardic tradition wane (even in Wales) and with it, the festival. Yet, it never vanished completely. In small towns and villages, poets and musicians still came together to compete for laurels and acclaim. Starting in the nineteenth century (and moved from winter to summer) nationwide eisteddfodau were held in such places as Abergavenny, Cardiff, Aberdare, and Llangollen. Like Lord Rys, the wish to heal deep wounds and celebrate war's end was integral to the people of Llangollen who, in 1947, held their first International Eisteddfod. Every year since, the festival has welcomed thousands from around the globe with concerts, recitals, feasting, dancing in the street, and a message of peace. For six days in July, you'll be hard-pressed to find a more Dragon-friendly venue in all of Europe. And, should you fancy an experience more rock n' roll than traditional, drop by Llangollen in May for the Red Dragon Music Festival.

Whatever your musical tastes, you'll feel the air crackle with Ddraigish energy, for you are in Dragon country.

Epilogue

DRAGONS: OUR LAST BEST HOPE

The Universe is a hostile place. Not by active intent, but by nature. And no one has known this as long or as well as Dragons.

Ever since their minute and Paleozoic ancestors fled from much larger carnivores, Dragons have known the Universe to be dangerous and forbidding. That they survived against odds we can hardly imagine, odds that took out all those larger carnivores, was nothing short of miraculous. Meteors fell, air and water turned toxic, and still they survived. They grew and evolved; they took

to the skies, became fire breathers and venom spitters, longer-lived than Methuselah and wiser than a thousand Solomons. They became Dragons: master/mistresses of all they surveyed. And save for the occasional natural cataclysm or rare terror bird with a death wish targeting newborn dragonlets, they had nary a care in the world. Despite the inherent cruelty of life and death, there was balance in this primordial Eden. Dragons—brazen, essential Dragons—helped keep that balance.

Human beings changed that balance. It didn't happen overnight; ours is a long, complicated relationship. When our species was young, our numbers few, it took all we had just to make it through the night to the rising dawn. In this nascent state, we were, as Jorge Luis Borges wrote, "as ignorant of the meaning of the dragon as we are of the meaning of the universe" (Borges, *The Book of Imaginary Beings*, 1974). And yet, in that blessed ignorance, we were still able to look up and see Dragons with reverence, respect, and no small measure of dread. They nourished our souls, both dark and light, and explained the unexplainable.

As we understood (or *believed* we understood) the world more, we found other explanations less dangerous and wild. In the process, we separated ourselves from our

fellow animals and started perceiving nature as something to be dominated and controlled. To that end, we stripped Dragons of their majesty and magic and let our Dragon reverence fade until only our fears remained. And fears breed violence faster than lemmings breed pups in summer. The enmity Dragons felt swirling round them was no longer natural. It was human and had deliberate, malicious intent. Dragons were there to be fought and killed, demonized and hated. "For the good of mankind," of course. We turned them into horrific icons of slavering death, and along the way, lost a Dragon-sized piece of our humanity.

We need to get it back. And to do that, we need Dragons. Now.

The world is in existential trouble and we put her there. Our avarice, stupidity, and get-them-before-they-get-us tribalism have set this remarkable blue orb and all her denizens on a path to annihilation. We've harmed land, sea, and air in unimaginable, possibly irreparable ways. The planet is warming, ice caps are melting, seas rising. We're erasing rainforests and wetlands; species by the hundreds—including Dragons—are going extinct every day. Even the Great Barrier Reef, its first polyps budding some eighteen million years ago, might be dead in a matter of years. And then there is the devastation we inflict upon our own kind in the name of gods, greed, and world-blinding vengeance.

Dragons weep—Earth is their home, too. They remember (some first-hand) better times, the balanced times. They have witnessed more loss than we can imagine. Their grief is palpable. So too, amazingly, is their hope. And in its aura, despite past wrongs and a history soaked in blood, they've found a way to believe in us, in our humanity ... fractured though it may be.

The truth the Dragons know (and which some of us are just discovering) is that Dragons—large, calid-breathed, cloud-dancing Dragons—are the first and last test of both our imagination and our belief. Of our reason and humility. We need Dragons to know passion and dreams and the fierce kindness we so often neglect. All those things we say make us human. We need them to be, as

> Dragons—large, calid-breathed, cloud-dancing Dragons—are the first and last test of both our imagination and our belief. Of our humanity.

Sir Terry Pratchett said, "the place where the falling angel meets the rising ape" (Pratchett, *Hogfather*, 2014).

Against the odds, they've found a way to come back to us. Tentatively at first, and then with growing gusto, they welcomed overtures—spiritual, creative, and scientific—of dracophiles near and far. When the world needs them most, needs lessons only Dragons can teach, when we need to be the best and most caring humans we can possibly be, they've come back. Impeccable timing, as always.

Will it be enough? I don't know. I do know that, as Joseph Campbell suggested, if we want to change the world, we have to change the metaphor (Oxford, 1980). Dragons are one whopping great metaphor. I know that if we embrace them in all their glory and wisdom, our chances improve. Our species improves. I do know they are a hope we can hold onto.

Because, in the final analysis, we're all bound up together. Our needs, reasoned and marvelous, are mutual things. And, if we need Dragons to be human, might not Dragons then need humans to be Dragon?

Should you prefer to live in ignorance and fear and insist on seeing Dragons as hostile, invasive influences on the planet while the planet crumbles around us, you are

missing the big picture. You are closing your eyes to the natural world—of which, like it or not, we are part. You might as well be standing on the back of a Dragon, trolling for geckos.

Best hold on tight. It's time to fly.

epilogue

BIBLIOGRAPHY

Anonymous and Francis B. Gummere. *Beowulf: The Harvard Classics, Vol. 49*. New York: P.F. Collier & Son, 1910.

Bissell-Thomas, J. *The Dragon Green*. London: Robert Hale Ltd., 1936.

Borges, Jorge Luis. *The Book of Imaginary Beings*. New York: Penguin Books, 1974.

Buchman, Dian Dincin. *Herbal Medicine*. New York: Wing Books / Random House, 1996.

Carson, Rachel. *The Sense of Wonder*. New York: Harper, 1998. First published 1965.

Conway, D.J. *Magical Mystical Creatures*. St. Paul, MN: Llewellyn Publications, 2001.

Cunningham, Scott. *Encyclopedia of Magical Herbs*. St. Paul, MN: Llewellyn Publications, 1996.

de Groot, J.J.M. *The Religion of the Chinese*. New York: Macmillan Company, 1910.

de Visser, M.W. *The Dragon in China and Japan*. Amsterdam: Johannes Muller, 1913.

Dickinson, Peter. *The Flight of Dragons*. New York: Harper & Row, 1979.

Gardner, John. *Grendel*. New York: Vintage, 1989.

Holy Bible, King James Version. New York: Meridian/Penguin, 1974.

Ingersoll, Earnest. *Dragons and Dragon Lore*. Lexington, KY: Forgotten Books, 2007.

Johnsgard, Paul, and Karin Johnsgard. *A Natural History of Dragons and Unicorns*. New York: St. Martin's Press, 1982.

Le Guin, Ursula K. Earthsea Trilogy. New York: Bantam Books, 1972.

———. *The Farthest Shore*. New York: Bantam Books, 1972.

MacKenzie, Shawn. *Dragons for Beginners*. Woodbury, MN: Llewellyn Publications, 2012.

———. *The Dragon Keeper's Handbook*. Woodbury, MN: Llewellyn Publications, 2011.

Matthews, John, and Caitlin Matthews. *The Element Encyclopedia of Magical Creatures*. London: Harper Element, Harper Collins Publishers, 2005.

Nietzsche, Friedrich. Translated by Judith Norman. *Beyond Good and Evil*. New York: Cambridge University Press, 2001. First published 1886 by C.G. Naumann (Leipzig).

Oxford Dictionary of Quotations, Third edition. New York: Oxford University Press, 1980.

Phillpotts, Eden. *A Shadow Passes*. Lexington, KY: Forgotten Books, 2012. First published 1918 by Cecil, Palmer & Hayward (London).

Pratchett, Terry. *Hogfather*. New York: Harper Collins, 2014. First published 1996 by Victor Gollancz (London).

———. *Reaper Man*. New York: Harper Collins, 1991.

Prince, J. H. *Languages of the Animal World*. New York: Thomas Nelson Inc., 1975.

Rose, Carol. *Giants, Monsters & Dragons*. New York: W.W. Norton & Co., 2000.

Saint-Exupéry, Antoine de. *The Little Prince*. New York: Harbrace Paperbound Library, 1971. First published 1943 by Reynal & Hitchcock (New York).

Simpson, Jacqueline. *British Dragons*. Hertfordshire, UK: Wordsworth Editions Limited, 2001.

Tedlock, Dennis, trans. *Popol Vuh*. New York: Touchstone Books, 1996.

Tolkien, J.R.R. *The Hobbit*. New York: Ballantine Books, 1970. First published 1937 by Allen & Unwin (London).

———. *The Lord of the Rings*. New York: Houghton Mifflin, 1994. First published 1954–55 by Allen & Unwin (London).

Television/Internet References

Game of Thrones. "Home." Season 6, Ep. 2. Directed by Jeremy Podeswa. Written by George R.R. Martin and David Benioff. HBO. May 1, 2016.

Kant, Immanuel Kant. "What is Enlightenment?" 1784. http://cnweb.cn.edu/kwheeler/documents/What_is_Enlightenment.pdf/.

Webster, Noah. ed. *American Dictionary of the English Language 1828*. http://www.Webstersdictionary1828.com/.